Intersectionality and Comparative Antidiscrimination Law

# Comparative Discrimination Law



Volumes published in this Brill Research Perspectives title are listed at *brill.com/rpcd*

# Intersectionality and Comparative Antidiscrimination Law

*The Tale of Two Citadels*

*By*

Shreya Atrey

BRILL

LEIDEN | BOSTON

This paperback book edition is simultaneously published as issue 4.1 (2020) of *Comparative Discrimination Law*, DOI:10.1163/24522031-12340008.

Library of Congress Control Number: 2020940063

Typeface for the Latin, Greek, and Cyrillic scripts: "Brill". See and download: brill.com/brill-typeface.

ISBN 978-90-04-38284-8 (paperback)
ISBN 978-90-04-38286-2 (e-book)



This book is printed on acid-free paper and produced in a sustainable manner.

# Contents

# Intersectionality and Comparative Antidiscrimination Law

*The Tale of Two Citadels*

*Shreya Atrey*
University of Oxford, UK
*shreya.atrey@conted.ox.ac.uk*

## Abstract

This volume in the Brill Research Perspectives in Comparative Discrimination Law addresses intersectionality from the lens of comparative antidiscrimination law. The term 'intersectionality' was coined by Kimberlé Williams Crenshaw in 1989. As a field, intersectionality has a longer history, of nearly two hundred years. Meanwhile, comparative antidiscrimination law as a field may be just over a few decades old. Thus, intersectionality's tryst with antidiscrimination law is a fairly recent one. Developed as a critique of antidiscrimination law, intersectionality has had a significant influence on it. Yet, intersectionality's logic does not seem to have infiltrated the logic of antidiscrimination law completely. Comparative antidiscrimination law continues to develop with intersectionality in sight, but rarely, in step. On the occasion of the 30th anniversary of Crenshaw's seminal article that coined the term in the context of antidiscrimination law, Shreya Atrey explores this irony. Her article provides a meta-narrative of the development of the two fields with the purpose of showing what appear to be orthogonal trajectories.

## Keywords

comparative law – discrimination – intersectionality – Crenshaw – grounds

## Preface

This volume is the eighth in the Brill Research Perspectives series concerning comparative discrimination law. This series addresses comparative discrimination issues both horizontally (overarching frameworks) and vertically (specific issues within discrimination law). Topics include unlawful discrimination

 | DOI:10.1163/9789004382862_002

on the basis of race, sex, religion, age, disability, gender, sexual orientation, as well as intersectionality – at national, regional, and international levels. Theoretical as well as more pragmatic approaches, such as the use of active measures to combat structural discrimination and proving discrimination claims with empirical evidence, are also explored. Law by its nature is bound by culture and language, and the effort in the series has been made to examine issues of discrimination from different jurisdictions.

This eighth volume in the Brill Research Perspectives in Comparative Discrimination Law addresses intersectionality from the lens of comparative antidiscrimination law. The term 'intersectionality' was coined by Kimberlé Williams Crenshaw in 1989. As a field, intersectionality has a longer history, of nearly two hundred years. Meanwhile, comparative antidiscrimination law as a field may be just over a few decades old. Thus, intersectionality's tryst with antidiscrimination law is a fairly recent one. Developed as a critique of antidiscrimination law, intersectionality has had a significant influence on it. Yet, intersectionality's logic does not seem to have infiltrated the logic of antidiscrimination law completely. Comparative antidiscrimination law continues to develop with intersectionality in sight, but rarely, in step. On the occasion of the 30th anniversary of Crenshaw's seminal article that coined the term in the context of antidiscrimination law, Shreya Atrey explores this irony. Her article provides a meta-narrative of the development of the two fields with the purpose of showing what appear to be orthogonal trajectories.

The editors welcome suggestions as to authors and jurisdictions outside those presented in the volumes to date. This series is to run for ten years of quarterly volumes, with the ambition to achieve a broad approach to comparative discrimination law issues.

## Part 1: The Tale of Two Citadels

There is perhaps just one way to inaugurate a discussion on intersectionality theory and antidiscrimination law, by citing the point in time the two fields first collided. It was 1989. The protagonist was Kimberlé Williams Crenshaw. In an issue of the University of Chicago Legal Forum was published, what was soon to become, a path-breaking piece: 'Demarginalizing the Intersection of Race and Sex: A Black Feminist Critique of Antidiscrimination Doctrine, Feminist Theory and Antiracist Politics'.[1] In that piece, Crenshaw critiqued the US

1 Kimberlé W Crenshaw, 'Demarginalizing the Intersection of Race and Sex: A Black Feminist Critique of Antidiscrimination Doctrine, Feminist Theory and Antiracist Politics' (1989) University of Chicago Legal Forum 139.

antidiscrimination law at the time and ended up calling that critique, 'intersectionality'. As we come to its thirtieth anniversary, lawyers can attest to the significance of that single piece that has become the leading starting point, footnote and reference for any conversation beyond the traditional mores of antidiscrimination law. It represents a rare feat for lawyers to have achieved the mythical consensus on the prominence of a theory, its origin, and its protagonist. And for a radical theory of its kind, it is no mean feat for intersectionality either.

Yet, as one would expect, the consensus is somewhat facile. There is no doubt that intersectionality has achieved prominence in antidiscrimination law and is frequently invoked as canonical within the field. But it appears that that is often no more than lip service and that intersectionality's main messages are far from absorbed as canon in legal terms. Intersectionality continues to be a hit-or-miss in courts, and while a section of scholarship invokes intersectionality quite dedicatedly, the rest remains decidedly non-intersectional. Similarly, while the 1989 piece is widely cited, it is equally the case that it is seldom correctly and fully read, and as part of a larger field of intersectionality studies. So also, while Crenshaw is rightly accredited for intersectionality, it is also true that intersectionality's supporters and detractors have both undermined the contribution, not only of Crenshaw, but of intersectionality's other proponents who appeared before and after 1989. Thus, despite what appear to be conciliatory gestures, antidiscrimination law's engagement with intersectionality is laden with contradictory messages.

The article explores this complex relationship. It is aimed at setting out the trajectories of the two fields – intersectionality theory and comparative antidiscrimination law, as they have developed in relation to one another. Their interaction over the last three decades shows that intersectionality has had a sure-fire influence on comparative antidiscrimination law. That influence is often measured in terms of judicial successes, that is, when a claimant wins an intersectional case in court. But that is just one way of measuring intersectionality's influence on antidiscrimination law. The increasing relevance of intersectionality in equality and antidiscrimination scholarship, confirms the growing influence of intersectionality furthermore. So, in one sense, intersectionality seems omnipresent. But seen in light of its theoretical and methodological insights, intersectionality appears to be present but dormant in doing the work it is supposed to in antidiscrimination law. This work is not only one of admitting conceptions of disadvantage beyond those that are unidimensional, but also infiltrating the very idea of disadvantage or discrimination in law with an intersectional understanding, such that intersectionality is no longer exceptional but central to antidiscrimination law. In the discourse of antidiscrimination law, this is still very much work-in-progress.

It is as if intersectionality and antidiscrimination law met at a point and continued to develop orthogonally from there. The sheer independence of their trajectories, despite the points of collision, including Crenshaw's exemplary intervention, tells a story of two related fields having developed as 'citadels'. In one way, citadels are fortified structures, difficult to penetrate. In another sense, citadels are meeting points or strongholds, providing common ground or refuge to people. The fields of antidiscrimination law and intersectionality seem to have evolved into citadel-like structures with respect to one another, each assured of its own logic and even open to possibilities of exchange from time to time. Yet, neither can be said to have ceded to the other, bringing down the walls and collaborating freely.

This is the story of this volume. It is divided into two parts. The first part takes Crenshaw's 1989 piece as the inflection point, with respect to antidiscrimination law. Taking cue from Ange-Marie Hancock's excavation of intersectionality's intellectual history, the part begins with sketching intersectional thinking in Black feminist thought for over two centuries prior to Crenshaw's intervention. This exercise helps situate Crenshaw's contribution in context. This is important because it helps understand intersectionality's substantive contribution to discrimination law better, including its appreciation of identities, disadvantage and appropriate responses. This understanding in turn comes handy in going over the period of heightened intersectionality critiques that urged variously for intersectionality's dilution, devolution, and even dissolution. These critiques unfolded over a long period and were followed by trenchant defences from intersectionalists. The critiques and the defences together reveal the fervent dynamism that defines intersectionality as a field. This part then represents a four-part developmental survey of intersectionality theory. The trajectory is not entirely linear and the attempt to make it seem so is only with the purpose of charting intersectionality's roots, longevity and main ideas, all via chronological pinpoints, to be able to estimate its relevance in antidiscrimination law today. I have shown elsewhere that intersectionality's trajectory of development in the US is similar to developments elsewhere, and in particular, the development of Dalit feminism in India.[2] But for the sake of feasibility alone, it may be useful to concentrate in this part on the US and its distinctive context in which intersectionality flourished, and which in turn influenced comparative antidiscrimination law greatly.

The second part of the article charts the development of intersectionality as against antidiscrimination law as manifest in – the doctrine of courts, as

2 Shreya Atrey, *Intersectional Discrimination* (Oxford University Press 2019) ch 2.

well as in comparative scholarship.[3] It traces the contradictory ways in which intersectionality is both present yet absent in comparative antidiscrimination law. Judicial and legislative engagements with discrimination based on more than one ground have coincided with the simultaneous developments in intersectionality scholarship since the 1980s. However, the developments in intersectionality theory and antidiscrimination doctrine do not necessarily mirror each other. While intersectionality is often cited, even engaged with, it is seldom translated into or realised in antidiscrimination law. Despite favourable appearances, the walled structure of antidiscrimination law appears far more impenetrable than imagined.[4] Examples from the US, UK, Canada and South Africa help make this case. Comparative antidiscrimination law inevitably refers to this limited range of jurisdictions herein, though similar comparative studies in other contexts also point to this conclusion.[5]

A few contextual remarks should help situate this narrative. This article does not make any normative claims as to how intersectionality or antidiscrimination law should be conceived or how should the citadels be cracked and rendered friendly. This has been done elsewhere.[6] This intervention, meanwhile, is a meta-narrative of the two fields alone and takes the reader through a journey from past to present, without trying to indicate the future. Given the occasion of the thirtieth anniversary of Crenshaw's seminal piece, its purpose is stocktaking, of developments that preceded the piece and that followed since. But it isn't simply for good timing that this stocktaking makes sense. It makes sense because the relationship between intersectionality and antidiscrimination law has gone through several phases of development, evolved, and is at a juncture

3 The distinction between these categories is somewhat artificial given the overlap in practice. Scholarship is deeply entwined with judicial decisions and both in turn work within the constitutional and statutory frameworks. The distinction then should be treated as more fluid than it purports to be, and hence useful only in organising the many distinctive ways in which antidiscrimination law and intersectionality transpire, even when the ways co-mingle.

4 The claim is descriptive alone and is not that the structure of antidiscrimination law is necessarily impenetrable.

5 See esp studies in EU and ECHR law, Sandra Fredman, EU Commission Report for the European network of legal experts in gender equality and non-discrimination, 'Intersectional Discrimination in EU Gender Equality and Non-discrimination Law' (2016) <http://ec.europa.eu/justice/gender-equality/document/files/intersectionality.pdf> (accessed 17 September 2019); Andrea Krizsan, Hege Skjeie and Judith Squires (eds), *Institutionalizing Intersectionality: The Changing Nature of European Equality Regime* (Palgrave 2012); Dagmar Schiek and Anna Lawson, *European Union Non-Discrimination Law and Intersectionality* (Ashgate 2011); Dagmar Schiek and Victoria Chege (eds), *European Union Non-Discrimination Law: Comparative Perspectives on Multidimensional Equality Law* (Routledge Cavendish 2008).

6 Atrey, *Intersectional Discrimination* (n 2).

where one can only proceed further with a clear idea of its developmental trajectory. It is thus a distinctly opportune time to be telling this story. And yet, it must be made clear that it is by no means the only possible narrative. The account of the two fields unfolding together (or not) is my own, and others may use exactly the same materials to arrive at a different account. They may even choose very different materials than those picked in this article. The fields are large enough that no single article or book can canvass the entire breadth of literature for each. This article works with some, and by no means all, seminal texts which are representative of the 'trajectories' and have thus played a role in how the fields have developed. What should be compelling enough in this review article is the descriptive account of the fields themselves, and the reader may well choose to draw their own conclusions from that. For example, they may find that the relationship between the two fields is actually mature, and not entirely citadel-like; or they may find that the two have barely coalesced, and that the citadel is permanently fortified. My own sense is that they have interacted, that too from the word go, and now continue to be perfectly cordial most of the times, but their ultimate union – one which acquiesces to the logic of the other – seems to elude.

## Part 2: Intersectionality

> 'Intersectional thinking suggests that race, class, gender, nation, sexuality, ethnicity, age, and other forms of social hierarchy structure one another.'[7]
> '[I]ntersectionality – the relationships among multiple dimensions and modalities of social relations and subject formations.'[8]
> '[I]ntersectionality [i]s an innovative and emerging field of study that provides a critical analytic lens to interrogate racial, ethnic, class, physical ability, age, sexuality, and gender disparities and to contest existing ways of looking at these structures of inequality.'[9]
> 'Intersectionality's intellectual project is thus twofold: an analytical approach to understanding between-category relationships and a project to

7 Patricia Hill Collins, *On Intellectual Activism* (Temple University Press 2012) introduction.

8 Leslie McCall, 'The Complexity of Intersectionality' (2005) 30 Signs 1771.

9 Bonnie Thornton Dill and Ruth Enid Zambrana, 'Critical Thinking about Inequality: An Emerging Lens' in Bonnie Thornton Dill and Ruth Enid Zambrana (eds), *Emerging Intersections: Race, Class, and Gender in Theory, Policy, and Practice* (Rutgers University Press 2008) 1.

render visible and remediable previously invisible, unaddressed material effects of the sociopolitical location of Black women or women of color.'[10]
'Intersectionality illuminates the dynamic of sameness and difference in patterns of group disadvantage based on multiple identities understood as a whole, and in their full and relevant context, with the purpose of redressing and transforming them.'[11]
'"Intersectionality" means the examination of race, sex, class, national origin, and sexual orientation and how their combination plays out in various settings. These categories – and still others – can be separate disadvantaging factors. What happens when an individual occupies more than one of these categories, for example, is both gay and Native American or both female and black? Individuals like these operate at an intersection of recognized sites of oppression. Do such cases require that each disadvantaging factor be considered separately, additively, or in yet some other fashion? Should persons who experience multiple forms of oppression have their own categories and representation, apart from those that correspond to the separate varieties of discrimination they experience? And what about the role of these "intersectional" persons in social movements such as feminism or gay liberation? Where do they belong? These are all questions that intersectional analysis attempts to address.'[12]

The trajectory of intersectionality depends on what one takes the term to be. Intersectionality could be located in multiple registers and across a host of disciplines, including, sociology, gender studies, literature, political theory, political science, anthropology, history, policy studies and law. But no discipline has a single coherent sense in which intersectionality exists. It is referred to variously as, an idea,[13] a concept,[14] a theory and praxis,[15] a research paradigm,[16] a

10 Ange-Marie Hancock, *An Intellectual History of Intersectionality* (Oxford University Press 2016) 33.
11 Atrey, *Intersectional Discrimination* (n 2) 37.
12 Richard Delgado and Jean Stefanic, *Critical Race Theory: An Introduction* (NYU Press 2017) 58–59.
13 Atrey, *Intersectional Discrimination* (n 2) ch 2.
14 Anna Carastathis, 'The Concept of Intersectionality in Feminist Theory' (2014) 9 Philosophy Compass 304.
15 Patricia Hill Collins and Sirma Bilge, *Intersectionality* (Polity Press 2016).
16 McCall, 'The Complexity of Intersectionality' (n 8).

heuristic and analytic tool,[17] a methodological approach and epistemological stance,[18] a metaphor,[19] an analytical and political orientation,[20] a field of studies etc.[21] There is something cross-cutting in all of these formulations, though it isn't clear what that is. The uses of the term, and its definitions, like those offered above, are diverse. In fact, intersectionality may be located even where the term is absent. Equally, it may be absent even when the term is deployed. Pinning down intersectionality to *one thing* – in a discipline, across disciplines, as a locution, in its usage, or definitionally, might be intellectually, both untenable and unintelligible.

Given the possibilities, not merely of failure, lawyers retreat to a more modest beginning to their intellectual engagement with intersectionality.[22] They follow another lawyer whose engagement with antidiscrimination law yielded the term intersectionality. Crenshaw thus becomes their chief interlocutor. In particular, her 1989 piece takes centre-stage. This is the path this article treads as well. It takes Crenshaw's intervention in 1989 as the inflection point for intersectionality, in not only coining the term, but also laying out the central critique of antidiscrimination law for lawyers to work with. But it isn't merely that the piece was a first in both these respects that it is relevant. As we shall come to see, that its argument is compelling, in its evidence and its analytic sensibilities, adds credence to the 1989 piece playing the role it does for lawyers.

This strategy though is fiercely contested. After several years of intersectionality having been treated almost monolithically as Crenshaw's brainchild, there has been a renewed call for accessing intersectionality more accurately and fairly, in terms of its origins and originators. Ange-Marie Hancock has responded to it. In her 2016 book, *Intersectionality: An Intellectual History*, she locates intersectionality's 'founding' in not only Crenshaw's but Collins' work in sociology which developed simultaneously with Crenshaw in the 1980s. In fact, Hancock takes us through over two centuries worth of intellectual thought that may be classified as intersectionality, showing that the sensibility was alive and thriving in Black feminist thinking long before either Crenshaw

17 Devon W Carbado, Kimberlé Williams Crenshaw, Vickie M Mays and Barbara Tomilson, 'Intersectionality: Mapping the Movements of a Theory' (2013) 10 Du Bois Review 303.

18 Sumi Cho, 'Post-Intersectionality: The Curious Reception of Intersectionality in Legal Scholarship' (2013) 10 Du Bois Review 385.

19 Ann Garry, 'Intersectionality, Metaphors, and the Multiplicity of Gender' (2011) 25 Hypathia 826.

20 Vivian M May, *Pursuing Intersectionality: Unsettling Dominant Imaginaries* (Routledge 2015) 3.

21 Sumi Cho, Kimberlé Williams Crenshaw and Leslie McCall, 'Toward a Field of Intersectionality Studies: Theory, Applications, and Praxis' (2013) 38 Signs 785.

22 A strategy, by no means, confined to lawyers alone.

or Collins' work appeared. Not only that, Hancock even shows 'the vast racial and ethnic diversity of intersectionality's foremothers'[23] spreading beyond Black feminists to women of colour generally, including Asian women, Latinas, Native American women in the US, indigenous women in Canada etc.

The choice of Crenshaw's contribution as the inflection point then requires greater justification. The first thing to clarify is that the choice does not exactly frame Crenshaw and her 1989 piece as the originator and the origin of intersectionality in any way. While Crenshaw did offer one of the first intersectional critiques of antidiscrimination law and called it as such, she did not invent the concept. Further, in Crenshaw's own words, her analysis was meant to be 'provisional'[24] and far from what could have been considered 'totalising'.[25] She drew inspiration from those who preceded her explicitly,[26] and has continued to draw on those who have developed intersectionality further.[27] A scholarly treatment of intersectionality may thus be an exercise in going back and forth from Crenshaw, at least for antidiscrimination lawyers, for whom her contribution has special relevance in the field. In designating her contribution as the pivot, one may merely be orienting themselves for intersectionality-related inquiries. That should not be seen as assigning intersectionality 'as hers', though they must show acute self-awareness of not doing so actually.

That then should help appreciate the scheme of this part of the article. First, it explores the trajectory of development of intersectionality-related thought, before the term was coined. Then, second, the coinage and its context are explored. Third, the development of the field is assessed in light of the numerous critiques levelled against intersectionality. And fourth, responses to those critiques are considered as a matter of reclaiming intersectionality in its most recent decade of development. Each of these 'phases' of development may be relevant to antidiscrimination lawyers both in understanding intersectionality itself and also the role it has played in legal matters of equality and non-discrimination over time. This will be considered specifically in the next part.

23 Hancock, *An Intellectual History* (n 10) 26.

24 Crenshaw, 'Mapping the Margins: Intersectionality, Identity Politics, and Violence against Women of Color' (1991) 43 Stanford Law Review 1241, 1244.

25 Ibid.

26 See the wealth of references to Black feminists in Crenshaw's 1989 piece (n 1) as well as her 1991 piece (n 24), including references to Sojourner Truth, bell hooks, Paula Giddings, Gloria T Hull, Phyliss Palmer, Angela Harris, Judy Scales-Trent etc.

27 See references in her two review articles (with others), 'Intersectionality: Mapping the Movements of a Theory' (n 17) and 'Toward a Field of Intersectionality Studies' (n 21), to Nira Yuval-Davis, Ange-Marie Hancock, Anna Carastathis, Nikol Alexander-Floyd, Kelly Coogan-Gehr, Nina Lykke, Jennifer Nash, Jasbir Puar etc.

### 2.1 *Before Crenshaw*

Few antidiscrimination lawyers would think of intersectionality as something existing prior to Crenshaw, i.e. before 1989. But intersectionalists would often go back in time to trace the idea, its theory, its mobilisation and practice as far back as the nineteenth century. A common starting point is Sojourner Truth's blazing speech from 1851. Truth, a Black woman and a former slave, knew the reality of her sisters all too well. But she was alone and daring when she decided to voice their condition at a rally for women's rights in Ohio. Pushed out by white men who questioned whether she was a woman, by white women who did not deem her fit to represent their cause for suffrage, and Black men who treated Black women's rights as secondary, Truth was extraordinary in her courage to deliver a speech which is worth quoting from:

> ... Well, children, whar dar is so much racket dar must be something out o' kilter. I tink dat 'twixt de niggers of de Souf and de women at de Norf all a talkin 'bout rights, de white men will be in a fix pretty soon. But what's all dis here talkin' 'bout? Dat man ober dar say dat women needs to be helped into carriages, and lifted ober ditches, and to have de best places ... and ain't I a woman? Look at me! Look at my arm! ... I have plowed, and planted, and gathered into barns, and no man could head me – and ain't I a woman? I could work as much as any man (when I could get it), and bear de lash as well – and ain't I a woman? I have borne five children and I seen 'em mos all sold off into slavery, and when I cried out with a mother's grief, none but Jesus hear – and ain't I a woman?[28]

Truth spoke about Black men and white women's claims to equal rights with white men, and their obliviousness, even outright rejection, of equality for Black women. She questioned the white men who believed her too weak to exercise freedom and equal rights (to vote). She reminded them of Black women's hard labour which equalled that of Black men but surpassed both theirs and white women's labour in that they faced unparalleled sexual and reproductive exploitation as slaves. With this, Truth established the quintessential line of reasoning which was to characterise intersectionality in years to come: of comparisons between similar yet different position of Black women and the positions of Black men, white women and white men. Frances Ellen Watkins Harper, Harriet Jacobs, Mary Church Terrell and Amanda Berry Smith, all Black female activists, advocated for equal rights in much the same terms throughout nineteenth century. Almost forty years later in 1892, Anna Julia Cooper was

---

28 Bell Hooks, *Feminist Theory: From Margin to Center* (2nd edn, SEP 2000) 214–215.

the first Black women to repeat this message in an assuredly academic voice in her book, *A Voice from the South.* Cooper urged Black women to find their distinctive voice through education, and to assert it as different from that of Black men and white women, and valuable for both feminist and anti-racist struggles.

Many of these names have now been brought back from obscurity and are frequently cited as having led the charge of intersectional thinking early on. But Hancock goes further back and in fact traces intersectionality in Maria Miller Stewart's *Religion and the Pure Principles of Morality* published in 1830.[29] Stewart spoke of the unique challenges faced by Black women, including sexual violence. She showed the same disappointment as others later, with Black men and white women in failing to include and advocate for Black women in their liberation movements. She thus exhorted Black women to challenge their exploitation in both individual and structural ways.[30]

It was this formidable history of activism and advocacy that came to define the period of fervent activity in intersectional thought. It may be accurate to pin down this period to the last fifty years. Thus, the passion for intersectionality grew rapidly at first in the 1970s.[31] Combahee River Collective issued its statement in 1977, which reflected its rich lineage and comparative methodology:

> Black, other Third World, and working women have been involved in the feminist movement from its start, but both outside reactionary forces and racism and elitism within the movement itself have served to obscure our participation ... It was our experience and disillusionment within these [Black] liberation movements, as well as experience on the periphery of the white male left that led to the need to develop a politics that was antiracist, unlike those of white women, and antisexist, unlike those of Black and white men.[32]

Combahee did not just stop there. They extended intersectional framings to sexuality and class, pointing to the need for Black feminism to speak to both, and beyond race and sex, in order to understand the complexity of oppression suffered by Black women. But their concerns even went beyond Black women

29 Hancock, *An Intellectual History* (n 10) 30.

30 See Marilyn Richardson (ed), *Maria W. Stewart, America's First Black Woman Political Writer* (University of Indiana Press 1987).

31 See Joyce A Ladneh, *Tomorrow's Tomorrow: The Black Woman* (Anchor Books 1972).

32 Combahee River Collective, 'A Black Feminist Statement' in Gloria Hull, Patricia Bell Scott and Barbara Smith (eds), *In All the Women Are White, All the Blacks Are Men, but Some of Us Are Brave: Black Women's Studies* (Feminist Press 1977) 13–22.

and towards 'combat[ing] the manifold and simultaneous oppressions that all women of color face'.

In the same year, Signs carried Dianne K Lewis' critique of the women's liberation movement which usually focussed 'exclusively upon the effects of sexism' and thus had 'limited applicability to minority women subjected to the constraints of both racism and sexism'.[33] She was relying on similar analyses that had been steadily voiced by Black feminists throughout the 1970s.[34] Indeed, 1970s was a period of real mobilisation. The first conference of the National Black Feminist Organization took place in 1973. The Black Women Organized for Action was also inaugurated in 1973. The League of Black Women, Black Women Concerned, National Black Women's Political Leadership Caucus, and Sisters Getting Ourselves Together, all sprouted on the US map during this time.[35] Activists, like academics, contributed not only to praxis but to the theorisation of Black women's position. In fact, there was never quite the distinction between the two, at least for Black feminism and intersectionality. Thus, one of the most cited pieces from this period remains 'Double Jeopardy' by Frances Beal, a prominent activist and New York Coordinator of the SNCC Black Women's Liberation Committee.[36] Another prominent crossover is Audre Lodre's 1978 piece 'The Transformation of Silence into Language and Action' which was equally poetic as it was action-oriented in rendering visible the hitherto invisible reality of Black women.[37]

The central theme of these academic and activist endeavours was the comparison of Black women's position in the US with that of Black men and white women. The purpose was to highlight their distinct experience of oppression, which failed to make stories of sexism and racism. They emphasised their

33 Diane K Lewis 'A Response to Inequality: Black Women, Racism, and Sexism' (1977) 3 Signs 339.

34 Amongst the plethora of literature Lewis cited were, Linda J M LaRue, 'Black Liberation and Women's Lib' (1970) 8 Transaction 59; Jean Cooper, 'Women's Liberation and the Black Woman' (1971) 63 Journal of Home Economics 521; Toni Cade (ed), *The Black Woman* (Signet Books 1970); Mae C King, 'The Politics of Sexual Stereotypes' (1973) 4 Black Scholar 12; Inez Smith Reid, *"Together" Black Women* (Third Press 1972); Geraldine Rickman, 'A Natural Alliance: The New Role for Black Women' (1974) 6 Civil Rights Digest 62; Pauli Murray, 'The Liberation of Black Women' in Jo Freeman (ed), *Women: A Feminist Perspective* (Mayfield Publishing 1975); Phyl Garland, 'Builders of a New South' (1966) 21 Ebony; Gerda Lerner (ed), *Black Women in White America: A Documentary History York* (Random House, Pantheon Boo 1972).

35 Diane K Lewis, 'A Response to Inequality: Black Women, Racism, and Sexism' (1977) 3 Signs 339, 340.

36 Frances Beale, 'Double jeopardy: To be Black and Female' (1971) reprinted in (2008) 8 Meridians 166.

37 See Audre Lorde, *Sister Outsider: Essays and Speeches* (Crossing Press 1984).

shared experiences but highlighted the experiences that were their own. For example, like white women, Black women were bound by their households and homework, yet, they were also bound by households of white women by whom they were exploited. At the same time, they were sexually exploited both by Black men and white men, though they did share much of the racism faced by Black men, in social, political, economic and cultural terms. While Blacks were disproportionately poor, Black women were poorer than Black men, paid less, if at all, for equal work. Thus, much of the analysis was embedded in the material conditions of Black women's position, integrating class with race and gender concerns. Characteristic of this is Bonnie Thornton Dill's 1979 piece in Signs.[38] Assimilating the Black feminist thought that preceded her,[39] Dill showed how 'a historical tradition of work forms an essential component in the lives of Afro-American women'.[40] Dill particularly showed how conceptions of Black women's work had been subsumed in notions of Black culture rather than appreciating distinctions between culture and social class. She argued that it was only the intersection of Black culture *and* social class taken together, that defined Black women's position. Thus, conceptions of femininity (or lack thereof) had to be juxtaposed against the history of slavery and exploitation at farms, factories and households alike.

The 1980s consolidated the gains made in 1970s. bell hooks' *Ain't I A Woman*[41] and Angela Y Davis' *Women, Race and Class*[42] were both published in 1981. In their book-length analyses, they punctured the myths surrounding Black women, from their 'sexual promiscuity' to 'matrilineal proclivities', and brought forth a sophisticated reality of Black women's condition in the US, from slavery through to the liberation movements in the twentieth century. At the centre of their efforts was a historical restatement of the Black female slave, whose reality had been steadily misrepresented, undermined or simply forgotten. This was important because the historical myths surrounding Black women continued to shape their reality in powerful ways. Imagined as controlling and domineering, they were constructed as less oppressed in studies of slavery.[43] It

38 Bonnie Thornton Dill, 'The Dialectics of Black Womanhood' (1979) 4 Signs 543.

39 Dill cites the following in particular for her work/class oriented analysis: Delores Aldridge, 'Black Women in the Economic Marketplace: A Battle Unfinished' (1975) 21 Journal of Social and Behavioral Scientists 48; Jacqueline Jackson, 'Family Organization and Ideology' in Kent Miller and Ralph Dreger (eds), *Comparative Studies of Blacks and Whites in the United States* (Seminar Press 1973).

40 Dill, 'The Dialectics of Black Womanhood' (n 38) 543.

41 bell hooks, *Ain't I a Woman: Black Women and Feminism* (South End Press 1981).

42 Angela Y Davis, *Women, Race and Class* (Vintage 1981).

43 For example, Davis cites the "Moynihan Report", 'directly linked the contemporary social and economic problems of the Black community to a putatively matriarchal family

was not possible to understand or alleviate their oppression unless their history was told anew. Thus, both hooks and Davis presented extensive studies of Black female slaves who were worked as brutally as their male counterparts, but also suffered systematic sexual abuse, including exploitation of their reproductive roles as 'breeders'[44] of another generation of slaves.[45] Their farm or factory work kept them from nursing their offspring, and even when pregnant or convalescent, were beaten, flogged and raped. Black women were not considered women, workers, mothers, or feminine at all; attributes otherwise available to white women. Yet, they performed on par domestically, in charge of cooking, cleaning and sewing, and available to men sexually no matter their sexual health. Their domestic labour was gendered and sexualised as it were for white women, though they were far from pedestaled for the performance of this work since they were just not considered women. They were *simply* slaves, but clearly in both a similar and different way than Black men. Their contradictory and complex position then was important in understanding their oppression today, defined by the continuing similarities and differences between their position and other oppressed groups like white women and Black men.

For antidiscrimination lawyers, Elaine W Shoben's article 'Compound Discrimination'[46] is of special significance. Appearing in 1981, it was one of the first systematic critiques of employment discrimination law in the US from the perspective of 'compound discrimination, that is, discrimination based on a combination of protected characteristics – such as race and sex – rather than single protected characteristics – such as race alone or sex alone.'[47] She distinguished compound discrimination from 'double discrimination' where 'no discriminatory effect [was] attributable to race alone or to sex alone.'[48] Shoben sifted through sixteen years of jurisprudence under Title VII of the Civil Rights Act of 1964, and showed how it had erroneously excluded claims based on more than one ground.[49] She argued that both the logic and the legislative

structure. "In essence," wrote Daniel Moynihan, the Negro community has been forced into a matriarchal structure which, because it is out of line with the rest of the American society, seriously retards the progress of the group as a whole and imposes a crushing burden on the Negro male and, in consequence, on a great many Negro women as well.' Ibid., ch 1.

44 Ibid.

45 Hooks (n 41) ch1; Davis (n 42) ch 1.

46 Elaine W Shoben, 'Compound Discrimination: The Interaction of Race and Sex in Employment Discrimination' (1981) 55 New York University Law Review 793.

47 Ibid.

48 Ibid. 796.

49 See for example, Shoben in footnote 5 of her article, identified a whole host of cases of 'double discrimination'.

history of the law indicated otherwise, that compound discrimination should have been protected.

We now know that more of antidiscrimination law-specific interventions were to follow, but at the time, especially before the breakthrough availed by Crenshaw's piece, Shoben's piece was in a league of its own. Sure enough, it was well within a long trajectory of Black feminist and intersectional thought, but it was still a rare intervention couched in legal terms. Because even after Shoben's piece, much of the scholarship continued to focus on intersectionality in spaces other than law. For example, it extended to Third world feminisms in the US, as evident in the exemplary collection of over three dozen essays lead by Cherrie Moraga and Gloria Anzaldua published in 1979.[50] Evocatively titled *This Bridge Called My Back*, the collection explored the specific condition of Third world women and how it had been ignored in liberation movements far and wide.[51] It offered a unified Third world feminism as an alternative which they hoped would unite and ultimately alleviate the condition of all women of colour, and in fact all oppressed. The offering was made from the clarity of their realisation that all struggles were interdependent. Liberation for no group was possible until all were liberated.[52]

In 1986, an important analysis of liberating theories was defined in terms of monism, 'that one particular domination precipitates all really important oppressions. Whether Marxist, anarchist, nationalist, or feminist, these "ideal types" argue that important social relations can all be reduced to the economy, state, culture, or gender.'[53] This analysis of the liberating theories was later relied on not only by Crenshaw, but picked up soon after, for example, by Deborah King.

In 1988, King introduced the twin ideas of multiple jeopardy and multiple consciousness.[54] In line with the preceding Black feminist writing, King's analysis relied on an explanation of Black women's condition defined in terms of both their commonalities and differences with white women and Black men. The fact that they were disadvantaged *as women*, like white women,

---

50 Cherrie Moraga and Gloria Anzaldua (eds), *This Bridge Called My Back: Writings By Radical Women of Color* (Kitchen Table Press 1981).

51 Chandra Talpade Mohanty, 'Under Western Eyes: Feminist Scholarship and Colonial Discourses' in Chandra Talpade Mohanty, Ann Russo and Lourdes Torres (eds), *Third World Women and the Politics of Feminism* (Indiana University Press 1991).

52 See also to this point, Barbara Smith (ed), *Home Girls: A Black Feminist Anthology* (Kitchen Table Press 1983).

53 Michael Albert et al., *Liberating Theory* (South End Press 1986) 6.

54 Deborah K King, 'Multiple Jeopardy, Multiple Consciousness: The Context of a Black Feminist Ideology' (1998) 14 Signs 42.

and *as Blacks*, like Black men, and distinctly *as Black women* themselves, indicated a position of multiple jeopardy. But in a break from previous writing, for King, it was important to understand 'multiple' not as an additive idea signified in references to 'double' or 'triple' jeopardy invoked, for example, ten years ago by Frances Beale, Beverley Lindsay et al.,[55] but to 'several, simultaneous oppressions but to the multiplicative relationships among them as well.'[56] She relied on Angela Davis' 1981 work *Women, Race and Class* to make the point:

> In other words, the equivalent formulation is racism multiplied by sexism multiplied by classism. The sexual exploitation of black women in slavery is a historical example. While black women workers suffered the same demanding physical labor and brutal punishments as black men, as females, we were also subject to forms of subjugation only applicable to women. Angela Davis, in *Women, Race and Class*, notes, "If the most violent punishments of men consisted in floggings and mutilations, women were flogged and mutilated, as well as raped." At the same time, our reproductive and child-rearing activities served to enhance the quantity and quality of the "capital" of a slave economy. Our institutionalized exploitation as the concubines, mistresses, and sexual slaves of white males distinguished our experience from that of white females' sexual oppression because it could only have existed in relation to racist and classist forms of domination.[57]

King went on to critique the obviation of this understanding of multiple jeopardy in the 'monist' conceptions of three liberation movements: antiracist politics, feminism and class politics.[58] Going over two centuries worth of history of these movements, she showed how Black women were relegated to the margins of each, when politics was defined as concerning a single oppression at a time. Crenshaw followed a similar line of inquiry in her 1989 piece. But King's examination of class politics challenging economic deprivation and exploitation was both unique and exhaustive. She took the reader through the beginnings of trade unionism in the late 1800s, communist rising in the 1920s and 1930s, and the anticapitalist politics in the 1960s. The movements were prolific in challenging the devastating effects

55 Beale (n 36); Beverly Lindsay, 'Minority Women in America: Black American, Native American, Chicana, and Asian American Women' in Eloise C Synder (ed), *The Study of Woman: Enlarging Perspectives of Social Reality* (Harper & Row 1979).

56 King (n 54) 47.

57 Ibid. (references omitted).

58 Ibid. 51.

of industrialisation visible in urbanisation, ghettoization, low wages, overwork, lack of job security, dwindling job satisfaction, deterioration of health, and poverty. But each of these successive movements imagined these plights as embodied in a white male worker, married, and responsible for a family. Women and Blacks were both initially excluded not only from participation in the labour market but also from trade union membership. Gradually, these restrictions were eased, de jure and de facto from the beginning of the twentieth century. But the positions of the Black female worker did not yet improve. They were largely confined to occupations that were non-unionised such as domestic work and agricultural labour. In industrial occupations and as factory workers, they were continually denied union membership, considered neither on par with their Black male counterparts, nor similar in position to white women who were paid better and enjoyed better working conditions. They were prone to sexual harassment in these rather intimate and isolated spaces – in households and farms. Throughout the course of the different Left movements in the US, not much had changed by the 1980s when King came to write her critique. According to King, 'a major limitation of both unionism and radical class politics is their monist formulations, wherein economics are exaggerated at the expense of understanding and confronting other oppressions such as racism and sexism.'[59] With little substantive or strategic regard to their position, Black women's specific disadvantages remained invisible and entrenched. Other than by themselves, when they started incorporating material and class-related struggles in their advocacy. Combahee River Collective is a leading example of this and for King, it represented their appreciation of multiple jeopardy as defined by racism, patriarchy, capitalism and imperialism, all at once.

Finally, in 1988, the year when Crenshaw delivered the speech that later appeared as her 1989 piece, came the crystallised text on anti-essentialism by Elizabeth Spelman. *Inessential Woman* provided an exhaustive case to forever render the category of 'woman' heterogeneous and diverse. Spelman poured scorn over the methodological and epistemological manoeuvres in feminism that put the lives of white middle-class women at the logical centre of feminist inquiry.[60] For example, she showed how women's oppression, framed by mainstream philosophy and mainstream feminism, as being pedestaled, as good women, dependent and confined to their homes, was representative of a rather small section of women, who were white and middle class. That had nothing

59 Ibid. 69.

60 Elizabeth Spelman, *Inessential Woman: Problems of Exclusion in Feminist Thought* (Women's Press 1990) x.

to do with Black women in the US whose oppression was connected to their history as slaves, as fallen, depraved and overworked.[61] For both white and Black women, race played a role in how sexism was experienced. According to Spelman, the choice not to see white woman's oppression in racial terms, because 'a woman is not oppressed on account of her racial identity hardly leads to the conclusion that the sexist oppression to which she is subject can be understood without reference to her racial identity.'[62] Thus, the primacy accorded to women's sex, over and above other forms of disadvantage women suffered based on their race, sexuality, class, age, disability etc., was misleading, and rendered generic conceptions of 'women' or 'sex' meaningless.

This is just some of what went on before Crenshaw's 1989 piece debuted. In reality, so much was happening in and around Black feminist scholarship and indeed scholarship of women of colour, that it is hard to collate and connect every development. But the flavour of these developments was clearly one of transformation or social change. No matter the location of analysis or the categories under review, the united force of intersectionality scholarship before 'intersectionality' was neither just ontological, i.e. identity or Self-related, nor just epistemological, i.e. concerned with knowledge. Instead, it was resolutely goal-oriented and hopeful of upturning the status quo. Collins describes it best:

> the 1970s and 1980s were the heady days of intersectional scholarship, a time when the critical analytical lens of intersectionality was attuned to assessing significant social issues, thinking through the mechanisms of intersecting systems of power themselves, and/or trying to do something about social inequalities.[63]

### 2.2 *Crenshaw and Since*

It was in this background that Crenshaw's 1989 piece appeared. Her purpose was straightforward. She sought to critique three fields in their treatment of Black women – antidiscrimination law, feminist theory and anti-racist politics. She showed how Black women's disadvantage, based on both race and sex, was marginalised in the single-axis conceptions of sex and race in antidiscrimination law, and within feminist theory and anti-racist politics respectively. Crenshaw argued that Black women were excluded from 'sex' or the category of 'women' in both antidiscrimination law and mainstream feminism which were confined to white middle-class women considered to be oppressed on

61 Ibid. ch 5.
62 Ibid. 15.
63 Patricia Hill Collins in Dill and Zambrana (n 9) ix.

the basis of sex alone. Similarly, Black women were excluded from antidiscrimination law and anti-racist politics that considered the category of 'race' to be about Black men alone. Antidiscrimination law, feminism and anti-racist politics were thus conceived as protecting those privileged in every way *but for* their race *or* sex, but not *both* at once. Black women, for whom discrimination was based on neither sex nor race alone, fell through the cracks of all of these movements. Crenshaw explained the nature of such discrimination as:

> Black women can experience discrimination in ways that are both similar to and different from those experienced by white women and Black men. Black women sometimes experience discrimination in ways similar to white women's experiences; sometimes they share very similar experiences with Black men. Yet, often they experience double-discrimination – the combined effects of practices which discriminate on the basis of race, and on the basis of sex. And sometimes, they experience discrimination as Black women – not the sum of race and sex discrimination, but as Black women.[64]

This dynamic, of similarities and commonalities existing alongside uniqueness and differences, is what characterised the compounded nature of Black women's discrimination. According to Crenshaw, the 'failure to embrace the complexities of compoundedness [was] not simply a matter of political will, but [sic] also due to the influence of a way of thinking about discrimination'.[65] The problem was thus epistemic in nature – both in terms of failing to grasp the nature of discrimination and making it fit the unidimensional ways of thinking about discrimination. But Crenshaw's aim was not simply to have the nature of Black women's discrimination fit this unidimensional logic, but to subvert the very ways of conceiving discrimination as single axis at all. It was in reference to this particular aim that she used the term intersectionality for the first time:

> [The] problems of exclusion cannot be solved simply by including Black women within an already established analytical structure. Because the intersectional experience is greater than the sum of racism and sexism, any analysis that does not take intersectionality into account cannot sufficiently address the particular manner in which Black women are subordinated. Thus, for feminist theory and antiracist policy discourse

64 Crenshaw, 'Demarginalizing' (n 1) 149.
65 Ibid. 166.

> to embrace the experiences and concerns of Black women, the entire framework that has been used as a basis for translating "women's experience" or "the Black experience" into concrete policy demands must be *rethought* and *recast*.[66]

Crenshaw used two metaphors to recast our ways of thinking about discrimination:

> Consider an analogy to traffic through an intersection, coming and going in all four directions. Discrimination, like traffic through an intersection, may flow in one direction, and it may flow in another. If an accident happens in an intersection, it can be caused by cars travelling from any number of directions and sometimes, from all of them. Similarly, if a Black woman is harmed because she is in the intersection, her injury could result from sex discrimination or race discrimination.
>
> Imagine a basement which contains all people who are disadvantaged on the basis of race, sex, class, sexual preference, age and/or physical ability. These people are stacked-feet standing on shoulders-with those on the bottom being disadvantaged by the full array of factors, up to the very top, where the heads of all those disadvantaged by a singular factor brush up against the ceiling. Their ceiling is actually the floor above which only those who are *not* disadvantaged in any way reside. In efforts to correct some aspects of domination, those above the ceiling admit from the basement only those who can say that "but for" the ceiling, they too would be in the upper room. A hatch is developed through which those placed immediately below can crawl. Yet this hatch is generally available only to those who-due to the singularity of their burden and their otherwise privileged position relative to those below-are in the position to crawl through. Those who are multiply-burdened are generally left below unless they can somehow pull themselves into the groups that are permitted to squeeze through the hatch.

Both the metaphors were introduced in the context of antidiscrimination law. In the first, 'traffic' metaphor, Crenshaw questioned the tendency to reduce discrimination to a single cause. By placing Black women literally at an intersection with traffic approaching from all sides, she not only showed the difficulty in assigning the cause of injury, but also what being 'harmed' in this circumstance meant. The traffic metaphor thus alluded to the multi-causal

66 Ibid. 140 (emphasis supplied).

nature of Black women's discrimination *and* to its aggravated nature at the intersection.

In the second, 'basement' metaphor, Crenshaw exposed the limited nature of antidiscrimination law conceived as a 'hatch' to escape the hierarchical organisation of disadvantage. She considered it limited because it allowed only those at the top of the hierarchy, those who were disadvantaged *but for* their race or sex, to escape. Those who were multiply disadvantaged were left behind unless exceptions were made. This was a design critique. Crenshaw was appraising the limitations of, what she called, 'the dominant framework of discrimination', as running along a single-axis alone and thus serving only those who were at the top of the basement, i.e. who were *singly* disadvantaged. But in another way, Crenshaw was also alluding to the hierarchical nature of antidiscrimination law, hinting at the ironic situation wherein laws meant to remedy discrimination, ended up discriminating between different kinds of discrimination, and as against those whose disadvantage was, per the traffic metaphor, multi-causal and aggravated.

Crenshaw continued to develop this analysis further in her 1991 piece titled 'Mapping the Margins: Intersectionality, Identity Politics, and Violence against Women of Color'.[67] In an extended analysis, Crenshaw showed how the nature of violence against women of colour could not be grasped in reference to sex or gender alone, as it is frequently a result of intersecting patterns of sexism, racism, poverty, etc. Crenshaw described three types of intersectionalities that came to define such violence – structural, political and representational.

But just as Crenshaw was developing her intersectional analysis, others were developing their own around the same time. For example, published in 1989, Judy Scales-Trent's article, 'Black Women and the Constitution: Finding Our Place, Asserting Our Rights' described Black women's condition as 'not only additive, but synergistic'.[68] She argued for treating Black women as a distinct group protected under the US Constitution because:

> Black women posess [sic] two statuses which derive from attributes over which they have no control membership in the black race and membership in the female sex. The combination of these two statuses creates a new status, and because it is a combination of two degraded statuses, black and female, the new status is a particularly low-ranking one.[69]

67 Crenshaw, 'Mapping' (n 24).

68 Judy Scales-Trent, 'Black Women and the Constitution: Finding our Place, Asserting our Rights' (1989) 24 Harvard Civil Rights – Civil Liberties Law Review 9.

69 Ibid. 14 (references omitted).

Scales-Trent cited much evidence to make a case for the 'more terrible',[70] 'dual disability',[71] or the 'double stigma' and 'double burden' faced by Black women.[72] For instance, she cited the statistics related to devaluation in job titles with high concentrations of minorities in the New York State.[73] For minority men, the devaluation was of 1.59 salary grades, while for white women it was 1.95 grades. But for women of colour, the rate was 2.77 grades. Thus, the fact that 'black women are the lowest paid group in America today when compared to white women, black men or white men', that they face 'significantly higher unemployment rates than any of those groups' and that their poverty rates were 'higher than the poverty rates for white women and black men', provided ample force to the argument that Black women were worse off than others and hence needed not as much but *more* constitutional protection in the US than other groups.[74]

Similarly, Mari Matsuda's 1989 piece continued to develop the jurisprudential method of multiple consciousness.[75] Matsuda considered experiences and histories of the oppressed, otherwise dismissed in law as irrelevant, inconsistent or unreliable, as significant to the jurisprudential inquiry. While jurisprudence may yet continue to be informed by the consciousness of strict legalism defined by abstraction and detachment, the consciousness of the standpoint of the oppressed, involved both 'skilled advocacy … and the search for the pathway to a just world.'[76] Matsuda urged for the standpoint of the oppressed to be embraced not only by those who were oppressed but by one and all in terms of appreciating its details and concrete particulars. This shifting of consciousness was later elaborated upon by Angela Harris in 1990.[77] In 'Race and Essentialism in Feminist Legal Theory', Harris laid bare the ontological intricacies of 'Self' for those who were multiply disadvantaged, such as Black women. She consolidated their sense of Self or personal identity as ever constructed, an act of will and creativity, rather than something ordained or determinable.[78] For this, they may rely on categorisation along the lines of 'sex' and 'race', but such

70 Ibid. 9.
71 Ibid. 10.
72 Ibid. 34.
73 Ibid.
74 Ibid. 9, 23, 34–35.
75 Mari Matsuda, 'When the First Quail Calls: Multiple Consciousness as Jurisprudential Method' (1989) 11 Women's Rights Law Reporter 7.
76 Ibid. 9.
77 Angela P Harris, 'Race and Essentialism in Feminist Legal Theory' (1990) 42 Stanford Law Review 581.
78 See also Dorothy E Roberts, 'Racism and Patriarchy in the Meaning of Motherhood' (1993) 1 American University Journal of Gender, Social Policy & the Law 1. See also Patricia

categorisation must always be 'explicitly tentative, relational, and unstable'.[79] Harris was categorical, that categories need not be abandoned, but that they be rendered open and reflexive. Thus, she advocated for the terms 'women' and 'women's experience' to be let open to the voices of Black women and their experiences. This, she argued, was crucial both for the feminist as well as the legal method, and for their commitment to reflect and redress everyone's stories.

Chela Sandoval urged for scholars to adopt 'oppositional consciousness'.[80] She imagined it as a kind of 'topography' where subjects constituted themselves as 'resistant and oppositional subjects' from points which were different from those they were defined by the social order.[81] Sandoval described this as a typical method of 'self-conscious mobility of consciousness' adopted by third world feminists in the US who both identified and enacted such consciousness differentially.[82] Much of this differential playing out of consciousness was adapted from feminists like Moraga and Anzaldua who had conceptualised third world feminism in the US in the previous decades.

In a similar vein, Regina Austin's 'Sapphire Bound!' article urged minority feminist legal scholars to develop an experiential character of jurisprudence which infuses experiences of minority women into legal analysis.[83] Important to her was the grounding of such analysis in the material conditions which defined minority women. Further, this was particularly important for lawyers, because, as Austin explained:

> The world with which many legal scholars deal is that found within the four corners of judicial opinions. If the decisions and the rubrics they apply pay no attention to race, sex, and class ... then the material conditions of minority females are nowhere to be found, and the legal aspects of the difficulties these conditions cause are nearly impossible to address as a matter of scholarly inquiry. It is thus imperative that we find a way to portray, almost construct for a legal audience, the contemporary reality of the disparate groups of minority women about whom we write.[84]

---

J Williams, 'Alchemical Notes: Reconstructing Ideals from Deconstructed Rights' (1987) 22 Harvard Civil Rights-Civil Liberties Law Review 401.

79 Harris, 'Race and Essentialism' (n 77) 586.

80 Chela Sandoval, 'US Third World Feminism: The Theory and Method Oppositional Consciousness in the Postmodern World' (1991) 10 Genders 1.

81 Ibid. 11.

82 Ibid.

83 Regina Austin, 'Sapphire Bound!' (1989) Wisconsin Law Review 539.

84 Ibid.

This analysis had a distinctly ontological strain, even if it is working with theoretical and doctrinal materials.[85] Intersectionality was thus operating in several of these dimensions at once: ontological and epistemic. This becomes apparent in the work of Patricia Hill Collins.

In 1989, Collins, a sociologist, published her intersectional analysis in 'The Social Construction of Black Feminist Thought'.[86] Locating Black women's oppression within the interlocking systems of race, gender and class, Collins posited the Black feminist standpoint which self-defined such oppression via two components:

> First, Black women's political and economic status provides them with a distinctive set of experiences that offers a different view of material reality than that available to other groups. The unpaid and paid work that Black women perform, the types of communities in which they live, and the kinds of relationships they have with others suggest that African-American women, as a group, experience a different world than those who are not Black and female. Second, these experiences stimulate a distinctive Black feminist consciousness concerning that material reality. In brief, a subordinate group not only experiences a different reality than a group that rules, but a subordinate group may interpret that reality differently than a dominant group.[87]

Collins elaborated on the significance of the distinctive Black feminist standpoint in her path breaking text *Black Feminist Thought* in 1990. The Black feminist standpoint provided the independent and internal viewpoint of Black women that fed into the making of knowledge or thought that defined Black feminism. The long-standing activism of Sojourner Truth, Anna Julia Cooper, Ida Wells Barnett and Fannie Lou Hamer, was thus distinctive in self-defining the Black feminist standpoint, as well as, in creating and being a resource for the recreation of Black feminist thought as it continued to be developed in the twentieth century. The point of both was to understand the complexities of

---

85 This is preceded by other similar ontological accounts from law professors and their experiences as Black women, see, Patricia J Williams, *The Alchemy of Race and Rights* (Harvard University Press 1992); bell hooks, *Black Looks: Race and Representation* (South End Press 1992); Regina Austin, 'Black Women, Sisterhood, and the Difference/Deviance Divide' (1992) 26 New England Law Review 877; Dorothy E Roberts, 'Deviance, Resistance, and Love' (1994) 26 Utah Law Review 179.

86 Patricia Hill Collins, 'The Social Construction of Black Feminist Thought' (1989) 14 Signs 745.

87 Ibid. (references omitted).

oppression experienced by Black women. Oppression, for Collins, was social, structural, intersectional, and characterised by a matrix-like framework. She called this organisation of intersecting oppressions a 'matrix of domination'. She explained thus:

> The term matrix of domination describes this overall social organization within which intersecting oppressions originate, develop, and are contained. In the United States, such domination has occurred through schools, housing, employment, government, and other social institutions that regulate the actual patterns of intersecting oppressions that Black women encounter.[88]

The matrix of domination was thus composed of the complexity of intersecting oppressions defined in turn by the complexity of history, context and social structures within which power operated. According to Collins, there were four domains of interrelated power, namely, structural, disciplinary, hegemonic, and interpersonal, wherein: '[t]he structural domain organizes oppression, whereas the disciplinary domain manages it. The hegemonic domain justifies oppression, and the interpersonal domain influences everyday lived experience and the individual consciousness that ensues.'[89] Importantly, power was never about privilege or oppression alone. For Collins, matrix of domination had 'few pure victims or oppressors' and in fact, individuals derived 'varying amounts of penalty and privilege from the multiple systems of oppression which frame[d] everyone's lives.'[90]

This entire framework then, of matrix of domination, composed of intersectional oppressions, defined in the particular historical and contemporary context, in which power operated, made up Collins' sophisticated argument in *Black Feminist Thought*. It lodged her firmly as one of the 'foremothers' of intersectionality.[91]

Two things are notable in Collins' analysis. First, her intersectional analysis though organised around Black women in the US was not meant to be for them alone. It was important for her to remind us constantly that the Black feminist thought is one that applies more broadly to projects of social justice, and to all

88 Patricia Hill Collins, *Black Feminist Thought: Knowledge, Consciousness and the Politics of Empowerment* (2nd edn Routledge 2000) 227–228.
89 Ibid. 276.
90 Ibid. 287.
91 Hancock, *An Intellectual History* (n 10) 26.

oppressed.[92] Second, and perhaps to drive home this point, she extends her analysis to Black men, to show how their oppression is very much gendered and sexualised, and not simply a matter of race and class as often imagined. In fact, she saw experiences of Black men and Black women as specifically shaped by sexual politics, of ideas of Black masculinity and Black femininity.[93] Ideas about sexuality and class framed Collins' central thoughts as much as gender and race.

At this point, while different locutions and vocabularies like matrix of domination, multiple consciousness, oppositional consciousness etc. continued to be developed, so did references to 'intersections' or 'intersectional' forms of thinking beyond Crenshaw and Collins. Thus, in 1991, Angela Davis delivered a keynote wherein she pressed on the importance of using the category of Black women as central to all legal analysis. Davis argued that centering of Black women would allow men and those in positions of privilege to be 'challenged to discover how they will indeed benefit from a vantage point that represents the intersection of so many forms of injustice and the fusion of so many forms of struggle and strength.'[94] In turn, she pressed on Black women to organise their own advocacy around intersections of many movements at once:

> As women of color, you will be called upon to challenge racist, anti-Semitic, misogynist, and anti-gay violence alike. It is no easy task to construct secure bridges – or perhaps a more appropriate metaphor would be mediating intersections – between our movements as well as between the struggles of the courtrooms and the struggles of the community.[95]

Like Crenshaw, the suggestion to appreciate the intersections methodologically in legal analysis, and strategically, in our political organising, was based on the point of knowledge that Black women's position was something missing in our understanding of the world but that understanding was crucial in finding

92 Collins, *Black Feminist Thought* (n 88) 43 ('In a context of intersecting oppressions, Black feminism requires searching for justice not only for U.S. Black women, but for everyone'). She makes this point persistently in her later work too. For example, in *On Intellectual Activism* (n 7), Collins remarks: 'I remind you that the framework of intersectionality encourages an opening up of this question beyond the specific case of African American women. We need multiple cases, grounded within intersectional analyses that examine how this same question affects individuals and groups in a global context.'

93 Developed later comprehensively in Patricia Hill Collins, *Black Sexual Politics, African Americans, Gender, and the New Racism* (Routledge 2006).

94 Angela Y Davis, 'Keynote Address' (1991) 43 Stanford Law Review 1175.

95 Ibid. 1178.

solutions for a more equal and just world. Davis posited the dynamic of sameness and difference as the fulcrum of this understanding:

> We are also suggesting that our ability to discover commonalities in our conditions and to explore our cultural and class differences may result in some new ways of looking at the world. These new ways of looking at the world may assist all of us – all progressive women and men – in our common quest for progress and radical social change.[96]

Another similarity exists in Davis' use of the metaphor of Black women being 'at the very bottom of society' which matches Crenshaw's basement metaphor.[97] She too called for an engagement with the histories and contexts of Black women, and indeed all oppressed, as important to the jurisprudential method(s) as lawyers, a call previously issued by Matsuda, King and Harris, in the form of multiple consciousness.[98]

Similarly, in 1991, Paulette M Caldwell's 'A Hair Piece' used not only intersectional analysis but started to refer that analysis as 'intersectional' as such.[99] Caldwell's scathing critique of the 1981 New York Court's decision upholding the prohibition on wearing braided hairstyles,[100] was based on the central premise of intersectionality: that there was just no way to understand discrimination against a Black woman who wore her hair in braids, but to appreciate the 'interactive effects of racial and gender discrimination.'[101] She asserted:

> *Rogers* proceeds from the premise that, although racism and sexism share much in common, they are nonetheless fundamentally unrelated phenomena – a proposition proved false by history and contemporary reality. Racism and sexism are interlocking, mutually-reinforcing components of a system of dominance rooted in patriarchy ... *Rogers* is an exemplar of employment discrimination cases that involve black women's

96 Ibid. 1177.

97 Ibid. ('as women of color we have been touched by so many forms of oppression that we might well consider ourselves to be at the very bottom of society').

98 Ibid. 1178. See also, Adrien K Wing, 'Brief Reflections toward a Multiplicative Theory and Praxis of Being' (1991) 6 Berkley Women's Law Journal 181.

99 Paulette M Caldwell, 'A Hair Piece: Perspectives on the Intersection of Race and Gender' (1991) Duke Law Journal 365.

100 *Rogers v American Airlines* (1981) 527 F Supp 229 (SDNY).

101 Caldwell, 'A Hair Piece' (n 99) 366.

> physical image, negative stereotypes of black womanhood, and the intersection of race and gender.[102]

The metaphor of the intersection, *and* its central pivot of the dynamic interaction between mutually enforcing systems of disadvantage, both seem to have solidified during this time. More importantly, like Crenshaw, this was now being applied very specifically to antidiscrimination law. Thus, Caldwell's critique of *Rogers* was a critique of how antidiscrimination law operated without intersectionality, offering in the process, how it *should*:

> The distinct history of black women dictates that the analysis of discrimination be appropriately tailored in interactive claims to provide black women with the same protection available to other individuals and groups protected by antidiscrimination law. The *Rogers* court's approach permitted it to avoid the essence of overlapping discrimination against black women, and kept it from applying the basic elements of antidiscrimination analysis: a focus on group history; identification of recurring patterns of oppression that serve over time to define the social and economic position of the group; analysis of the current position of the group in relation to other groups in society; and analysis of the employment practice in question to determine whether, and if so, how, it perpetuates individual and group subordination.[103]

Caldwell's enunciation of 'the basic elements of antidiscrimination analysis' is a powerful antidote to the traditional mores of antidiscrimination law grounded in abstract forms of analysis removed from actual claimants and their reality. Kathy Abrams continued this analysis with respect to Title VII claims.[104] She questioned the aversion in antidiscrimination law to complexity that saw only people's disadvantage and as just running along a single axis. She considered complexity, or complex subjectivity as she called, more fundamental than often admitted, defining everyone's position in terms of privilege and subordination, though in no similar ways.[105] She found that while courts often acknowledged this position of complex subjectivity, they seldom offered an intelligible account of them.

102 Ibid. 371–372.

103 Ibid. 377.

104 Kathy Abrams, 'Title VII and the Complex Female Subject' (1993) 92 Michigan Law Review 2479.

105 Ibid. 2490–2492.

In the 1990s then, the direction of intersectional scholarship was gradually but firmly towards ever greater critique of antidiscrimination law. This was in addition to all the other directions of travel that were simultaneously being pursued in literature, sociology, anthropology, politics, etc. Intersectionality was thus developing prolifically, and the possibilities of engagement were vast. While many continued to develop intersectionality in significant ways, others had begun posing significant challenges to it. Especially outside the Black feminist circles, there was growing noise questioning the ways intersectionality was posited and performed. For example, Elvia R Arriola argued that intersectionality had limited purchase for groups beyond Black women.[106] She thus proposed her own 'alternative perspective of multiple intersectionality – a "holistic/irrelevancy" theory'.[107] This alternative perspective was based on the understanding that intersectionality did not 'reach discrimination occurring along intersections of non-traditionally recognized categories, such as homosexuality' and that questions of sexuality and gender could not be 'viewed in the way one traditionally thinks of race or even gender discrimination'.[108] Thus, multiple intersectionality was proposed as pushing forward Crenshaw's contribution by extending it to categories beyond the combination of race and sex.

Similar analysis followed from Francisco Valdes, Peter Kwan and Darren Hutchinson (independently).[109] Valdes, like Arriola, claimed that

106 Elvia R Arriola, 'Gendered Inequality: Lesbians, Gays and Feminist Legal Theory' (1994) 9 Berkeley Women's Law Journal 103, 128 ('Crenshaw's discussion of "intersectionality" is an extremely valuable contribution to the feminist critique of traditional methods of discrimination analysis. However, it fails to address the individual who experiences discrimination on the basis of multiple aspects of her identity. Traditional methods of analysis fail such an individual, and Crenshaw's theory remedies only those situations where traditionally recognized categories, such as race and sex, intersect in a particular social identity.').

107 Ibid. 108.

108 Ibid. 129.

109 Francisco Valdes, 'Sex and Race in Queer Legal Culture: Ruminations on Identities and Interconnectivities' (1995) 5 Southern California Review of Law and Women's Studies 25; Francisco Valdes, 'Queer Margins, Queer Ethics: A Call to Account for Race and Ethnicity in the Law, Theory, and Politics of "Sexual Orientation"' (1997) 48 Hastings law Journal 1293; Peter Kwan, 'Jeffrey Dahmer and the Cosynthesis of Categories' (1997) 48 Hastings Law Journal 1257; Darren Lenard Hutchinson, 'Out Yet Unseen: A Racial Critique of Gay and Lesbian Legal Theory and Political Discourse' (1997) 29 Connecticut Law Review 561; Darren Lenard Hutchinson, 'Ignoring the Sexualization of Race: Heteronormativity, Critical Race Theory, and Anti-Racist Politics' (1999) 47 Buffalo Law Review 1; Darren Lenard Hutchinson, 'Identity Crisis: "Intersectionality," "Multidimensionality," and the Development of an Adequate Theory of Subordination' (2000) 6 Michigan Journal of Race and Law 285; William N Eskridge, Jr., 'Outsider-Insiders: The Academy of the Closet' (1996) 71 Chicago-Kent Law Review 977; Mary Eaton, 'Homosexual Unmodified:

intersectionality's legal or doctrinal utility was limited on the basis that '"sexual orientation discrimination" [was] not formally prohibited by federal anti-discrimination statutes'.[110] This argument was that because intersectionality was premised on race and sex, categories that formally were protected from discrimination under Title VII, it was thus limited to them and could not necessarily be extended to categories that were not (yet) protected.

Kwan argued that intersectionality was in fact complex enough to capture other forms of disadvantage, but it was still limited by its 'discourse on race, gender, and to a large extent, sexual orientation … [which was] ironically one of uncritical intersecting autonomic categories.'[111] Kwan, unlike Arriola and Valdes, did not think that intersectionality was limited to sex and race or to Black women or to any set of identities for that matter. He recognised that 'what is distinctive about intersectionality is not so much the recognition of multiple identities in specific loci, but the separate political claim that this multiplicity calls for separate theoretical consideration *against the grain* of cultural and legal orthodoxy.'[112] Thus, it was the challenge to the hegemony of the dominant paradigms that was critical to intersectionality. Yet, Kwan thought that intersectionality was susceptible to the 'reductive trap' because:

> It is not just that intersectionality slighted issues of sexual orientation … but that by focusing, for example, on the particularities of black women's experience, intersectionality stands in danger of pushing to its margins issues of class, religion, and able-bodiedness, as well as issues of sexual orientation. Thus, without a more developed theory of how to "factor in" these issues, as Crenshaw predicted, intersectionality stands in danger of perpetuating the very dangers to which it alerted with regard to male dominance in racial discourses, and white supremacy in feminist discourses.[113]

But this 'factoring in' could not be done by intersectionality anyway. For Kwan, intersectionality's invocation of identities was too uncritical, reifying their use and ultimately splintering each 'individual' case of intersectional identity to just itself and thus reducing the possibility of using that category to say

Speculations on Law's Discourse, Race, and the Construction of Sexual Identity' in Didi Herman and Carl Stychin (eds), *Legal Inversions* (Temple University Press 1995).

110 Valdes, 'Queer Margins' (n 109) 1333–1335.

111 Kwan, 'Jeffrey Dahmer' (n 109).

112 Ibid. 1275.

113 Ibid. 1276.

anything meaningful about broader patterns of disadvantage. He thus offered 'cosynthesis' as an analytical theory for overcoming this:

> Cosynthesis offers a dynamic model whose ultimate message is that the multiple categories through which we understand ourselves are sometimes implicated in complex ways with the formation of categories through which others are constituted. A fully deconstructed understanding of categories must include this insight and go beyond static and autonomous notions of categories that stand alone or next to or within others, thereby multiplying the boundaries between categories.'[114]

Much in the same vein, Hutchinson proposed his multidimensionality framework as 'a substantive and conceptual extension and redirection of [intersectionality] literature.'[115] Hutchison, like others, testified to the significance of intersectionality in spearheading the movement for recognising the complexity of oppression, but questioned yet again the lack of analysis beyond patriarchy and racism and especially the lack of emphasis on 'the social meaning of sexual identity'.[116] Intersectionality thus created 'a false implication that only women of color experience multilayered subordination.'[117] But in fact, Hutchinson argued, 'multilayered experiences are "universal"'.[118] In order to appreciate it, he proposed multidimensionality as a methodology for analysing 'the impact of racial and class oppression (or other sources of social inequality) upon sexual subordination and gay and lesbian experience and identity and to cease treating these forces as separable, mutually exclusive, or even conflicting phenomena.'[119]

It was Kwan who had first urged moving 'post-intersectionality'.[120] Valdes too had declared Kwan's efforts at cosynthesis and Hutchinson's efforts at multidimensionality as going 'beyond intersectionality'.[121] Not much later, Robert S Chang and Jerome Culp Jr urged going 'past the intersection' and contributing to another discourse that may follow 'after intersectionality'.[122] These

114 Ibid. 1280.
115 Hutchinson, 'Ignoring Sexualization of Race' (n 109) 11.
116 Ibid. 11–12.
117 Ibid. 14.
118 Ibid. 16–17.
119 Hutchinson, 'Out Yet Unseen' (n 109) 640.
120 Kwan, 'Jeffrey Dahmer' (n 109) 1264.
121 Valdes, 'Queer Margins' (n 109) 1338.
122 Robert S Chang and Jerome Culp Jr, 'After Intersectionality' (2002) 71 UMKC Law Review 486, 490–491.

entreaties shared in common their central concern with intersectionality, even if their proposed solutions differed. The concern was with intersectionality's use of identity-categories. To them, intersectionality seemed to be restricted to the categories of race and sex, and to Black women in particular. But the concern went further. Which other categories were to be used and why? How far could one go on splintering categories? Was there anything of collational politics left if we splintered categories beyond recognition? Why did intersectionality use categories at all, instead of rejecting them wholly? These were the questions posed in the bout of early critiques that were to become 'all the rage' in the new millennium.[123]

### 2.3 *'Post-Intersectionality'*

The noughties saw intersectionality peak in two dimensions. First, intersectionality was firmly lodged in feminist theories and praxis and was no longer an 'outsider' idea. Feminists thus declared intersectionality to have triumphed. In 2005, Leslie McCall said that 'intersectionality is the most important contribution that women's studies, in conjunction with related fields, has made so far'.[124] Similarly, Kathy Davis saw intersectionality as a 'feminist success story' or having 'all the makings of a successful feminist theory', with its 'remarkable success in contemporary feminist scholarship'.[125]

Second, these accounts existed alongside a vociferous stream of intersectionality critiques. A range of problems were highlighted, and importantly, considered irresolvable. Intersectionality was thus simultaneously declared to have 'little more that it can now contribute.'[126] In this strand of literature, intersectionality appeared to have run its course and considered of limited avail as a theory, methodology, or tool for social movements.

It is then useful to unravel this tension within intersectionality literatures in the noughties. For this, let us return to McCall and Davis. Their declarations of intersectionality's success were not made in vacuum. In fact, both were writing cognisant of the backlash against intersectionality. McCall was particularly interested in responding to the methodological challenges to intersectionality that raised important questions about *how* intersectionality was to be wielded. In some ways, it was apparent what intersectionality did and what it could achieve, but for it to achieve the status of a 'theory', academics

123 May, *Pursuing Intersectionality* (n 20) 98.
124 McCall, 'The Complexity of Intersectionality' (n 8) 1771.
125 Kathy Davis, 'Intersectionality as Buzzword' (2008) 9 Feminist Theory 67.
126 Emily Grabham, Davina Cooper, Jane Krishnadas and Didi Herman (eds), *Intersectionality and Beyond: Law, Power and the Politics of Location* (Routledge Cavendish 2009) 4.

were particularly concerned as to how it were to be *done* at all, i.e. statistically, ethnographically, etymologically, etiologically, genealogically, by deconstruction etc. The lack of clarity in this respect seemed to demote intersectionality to the level of just another interesting idea, though nothing particularly rigorous. Some felt that its rigour thus needed to be culled out and (re)stated explicitly. For example, McCall proposed three approaches to working with intersectionality – anti-categorical, intercategorical and intracategorical complexities, each relying on methods of deconstruction, systems or relational analysis, and strategic and identity-based interventions, respectively. She thus classified intersectionality literature as existing in all these methodological domains and argued that the complexity of intersectionality could not be neatly reduced to a single methodology and that in fact that would defeat the purpose of intersectionality if it was. To her, it was the sheer fact of complexity of the social relations that intersectionality revealed that yielded itself to such complexity of methods. In a similar vein, Davis flipped intersectionality's 'alleged weaknesses' – its ambiguity and open-endedness – into what made it 'a good feminist theory.'[127] She chose not to resolve the debates over intersectionality's ambiguity or open-endedness. Instead, she chose to focus on processes of scientific activity, especially those through which specific theoretical perspectives become persuasive or on-trend with an academic audience.[128] Drawing on the work of Murray S Davis, she showed that theories that have mass appeal are not those that are true or coherent but those that appeal to a fundamental concern for many, and are in fact fluid and open to addressing the concern.[129] Thus, for both McCall and Davis, the fact that we cannot pin down intersectionality to a straightjacket, was something to be regarded with appreciation.

In 2008, S Laurel Weldon testified to this multi-approach reading of intersectionality.[130] According to her, there were at least two possible approaches: intersectionality-only and intersectionality-plus. While the former 'needlessly limits empirical investigation employing the concept and obstructs social structural analysis', the latter 'recognizes the possibility of multiple types of interactions among social structures, and permits the theorization

127 Davis (n 25).

128 Ibid. 69.

129 See Murray S Davis, 'That's Interesting! Towards a Phenomenology of Sociology and a Sociology of Phenomenology' (1971) 1 Philosophy of the Social Sciences 309; Murray S Davis, '"That's Classic!" The Phenomenology and Rhetoric of Successful Social Theories' (1986) 16 Philosophy of the Social Sciences 285.

130 S Laurel Weldon, 'Intersectionality' in Gary Goertz and Amy G Mazur (ed), *Politics, Gender, and Concepts Theory and Methodology* (CUP 2008).

and investigation of these different types of interactions'.[131] The difference lay in how the identity-categories and the context in which they transpired, were treated.

Similarly, in 2010, Choo and Feree provided at least three routes to understanding intersectionality theory and methodology – group-centered, process-centered, and system-centered.[132] While they found intersectionality to be underutilised in sociology, they hoped that 'all three tools can complement and enhance the specific purposes of the researcher by making analysis more effective.'[133]

Writing in a chiefly British context, Nira Yuval-Davis clarified a few more important things about intersectionality.[134] First, she clarified that the 'axes' or identities were not self-standing or isolated but forever enmeshed and constituted by one another. There was thus no point trying to think of pure categories of sex or race at all. Second, she seemed to consider the proliferation of axes or identities to be relatively unproblematic. She did not consider it a matter of simple signification or staking a claim to an identity, but rather a matter of understanding social power to be able to mobilise social struggles as a group or from a certain position.

None of these responses seemed to satisfy the critics, who steadfastly stuck to their disagreement, despite, ironically, also claiming to not undermine intersectionality. Chief amongst these remains Jennifer Nash's 2008 piece, 'Rethinking Intersectionality'.[135] She highlighted four concerns as contributing to what she saw as intersectionality's 'theoretical, political, and methodological murkiness': the lack of a defined intersectional methodology; the use of Black women as quintessential intersectional subjects; the vague definition of intersectionality; and the empirical validity of intersectionality. Not

131 Ibid. 218.

132 Hae Yeon Choo and Myra Marx Ferree, 'Practicing Intersectionality in Sociological Research: A Critical Analysis of Inclusions, Interactions, and Institutions in the Study of Inequality' (2010) 28 Sociological Theory 129 ('The first, emphasizes placing multiply-marginalized groups and their perspectives at the center of the research. The second, intersectionality as a process, highlights power as relational, seeing the interactions among variables as multiplying oppressions at various points of intersection, and drawing attention to unmarked groups. Finally, seeing intersectionality as shaping the entire social system pushes analysis away from associating specific inequalities with unique institutions, instead looking for processes that are fully interactive, historically co-determining, and complex.').

133 Ibid. 130.

134 Nira Yuval-Davis, 'Intersectionality and Feminist Politics' (2006) 13 European Journal of Women's Studies 193.

135 Jennifer C Nash, 'Re-thinking Intersectionality' (2008) 89 Feminist Review 1.

only Crenshaw's, but Nash read almost every other scholar's work, including Matsuda and Wing's, as useful but ultimately 'romanticiz[ing] and idealiz[ing] positions of social subordination.' In fact, the fulcrum of Nash's critique seems to be the focus on Black women that she considered too under-developed to make for a coherent theory. Limited to an analysis of subordination (not privilege) and limited to race and sex (not class, sexuality etc.), intersectionality was too narrow in Nash's estimation. Baukje Prins repeated this critique but from the perspective that Black women's example was perhaps too extreme to work with and to be generalisable and ultimately useful for the majority.[136] Lena Gunnarsson, took this critique a level further and dismissed not only intersectionality's reference to Black women's lives, but for that, intersectionality's unsophisticated understanding of identity itself, which was perhaps too focused on physical appearances.[137]

In any case, others seemed dissatisfied with the invocation of identities at all. Jasbir Puar and later Emily Grabham argued against intersectionality's view of identities as distinct at all, as if existing independently before they 'intersect'.[138] For them, intersectionality moved from the assumption that there was something like an essentialist identity that existed in a pre-intersectional state. It was the metaphor of *intersection* itself that seemed to exasperate these critics. A very similar critique continued to be voiced that saw intersectional identities as highly fragmented to the point of being relevant only at the level of the individual and having little to do with groups or serving as grounds for coalitional politics.[139] Thus, its focus on identity was considered too individualistic to yield itself to identity politics at a strategic or political level. In any case, it was argued that no major political gains could possibly be made with intersectionality invoking identity at all and thus failing to challenge the reification of identities per se.

---

136 Baukje Prins, 'Narrative Accounts of Origins: A Blind Spot in the Intersectional Approach?' (2006) 13 European Journal of Women's Studies 277. See also Wendy Hulko, 'The Time – and Context-Contingent Nature of Intersectionality and Interlocking Oppressions' (2009) 24 Affilia 44.

137 Lena Gunnarsson, 'A Defence of the Category "Women"' (2011) 12 Feminist Theory 23.

138 Jasbir K Puar, 'Queer Times, Queer Assemblages' (2005) 23 Social Text 121; Emily Grabham, 'Taxonomies of Inequality: Lawyers, Maps and the Challenges of Hybridity Social and Legal Studies' (2006) 15 Social and Legal Studies 5. See also Davina Cooper, *Challenging Diversity: Rethinking Equality and the Value of Difference* (Cambridge University Press 2004).

139 Amongst others, see, Lakshmi Arya, 'Imagining Alternative Universalisms: Intersectionality and the Limits of Liberal Discourse' in Grabham et al., *Intersectionality and Beyond* (n 126); Naomi Zack, Naomi, *Inclusive Feminism: A Third Wave Theory of Women's Commonality* (Rowman and Littlefield 2005).

The (ir)relevance of class analysis in intersectionality was another bone of contention. In 2001, Beverly Moran expressed that intersectionality 'leaves out factors that are at least as important to me as race and sex, in particular, the question of class.'[140] She did not substantiate how, though she did appreciate efforts of those who increasingly focussed on class analysis within intersectionality. Her main concern however was that intersectionality undercut concerns about culture. It was her belief that the category of Black woman, while potentially liberating, was oppressive after all, constructed to oppress and ultimately 'destroy our culture.'[141] As a category, it drove a wedge between Black men and women and thus Moran hoped, 'for the day when the phrase 'Black people' means more than Black men. When we as a people are allowed to have a culture that flourishes without the distinction of Black male and Black female that is at its root, a construction of the powers that have oppressed us for so long.'[142] Her response was thus different from that of intersectionalists who see Black women for who they are, and instead urged us, 'to look at Black people as a whole, as a unique culture that deserves respect and preservation.'[143] She thus issued a challenge for intersectionality: 'A challenge to take what our oppression has given us and use it to create something new that is ours alone, to create a critique of what we have become as a result of our oppression and a vision of what we can become when we leave behind our bondage.'[144] She believed in intersectionality's ability to achieve this ('I am sure that I will not be disappointed'[145]).

Yet, others have not been so sure in their critiques. For example, almost ten years later, Joanne Conaghan again critiqued intersectionality's apparently enduring neglect of class.[146] The thrust of her critique was twofold: (i) the legal roots of intersectionality in antidiscrimination law, most evident in Crenshaw's framing, limited its ability to transform into 'more effective analytical and strategic tools'; (ii) and the subsequent 'identity turn' in intersectionality scholarship (*pace* Grillo, West et al.) while transcending the legal realm, still did not

140 Beverly Moran, 'Keynote Address Delivered for the Journal of Contemporary Legal Issues Conference on the Future of Intersectionality and Critical Race Feminism' (2001) 11 Journal of Contemporary Legal Issues 691, 696.

141 Ibid. 697.

142 Ibid.

143 Ibid. 697–698.

144 Ibid. 699.

145 Ibid. 700.

146 Joanne Conaghan, 'Intersectionality and the Feminist Project in Law' in Grabham et al. (n 126).

speak to class which was *relational* not *locational* in nature (unlike race and gender). According to Conaghan:

> it is perfectly possible (and not unusual) to engage with processes and relations in the context of enquiries into identity formation. However, because law is embedded in a liberal individualist paradigm it is not an ideal site for this kind of interrogation. Hence the difficulties with according class any kind of legal significance.[147]

Davina Cooper elaborated on this systems/relational critique further. For Cooper, the way to understand the structure of inequality was to focus not on identity-categories at all, but the *processes* that shaped them and the resultant inequality. Like Conaghan, she conceived intersectionality's focus on (social) identity-categories, individually and as a group, as a far cry from this. Her suggestion, thus, was to treat intersectionality as a two-sided process: 'On one side is a *series* of different lenses. In each case, social life does not change but the interrelationship moving into focus does. On the other, intersectionality represents a series of conceptual travels.'[148] She delineated three kinds of conceptual travels: categorical mobility, dynamic routing, and relational saturation. Only the first one focussed on identity-categories, their formation, interaction etc. The second pointed to the mobile social dynamic of these identity-categories, and the last pointed to the power of inequality to shape social dynamics.[149] While these were not the only intersectional travels possible, Cooper posited them as signifying the sheer multiplicity of '*different* intersectional lenses and following different conceptual journeys.'[150]

Critiques of intersectionality ran abound in the noughties. May describes this trend as having taken the form of its 'own genre – a form so flourishing, at times it seems critique has become a primary means of taking up the concept and its literatures.'[151] That would have been true had the critiques just operated on their own. Yet, intersectionalists came back to crits with vehemence. This move, characteristic of the current decade, may properly be described as one of reclaiming intersectionality. The next section explores this.

---

147 Ibid. 30.

148 Davina Cooper, 'Intersectional Travel Through Everyday Utopias: The Difference Sexual and Economic Dynamics Make' in Grabham et al. (n 126) 308.

149 Ibid. 309.

150 Ibid. (emphasis in original).

151 May, *Pursuing Intersectionality* (n 20) 98.

### 2.4 *Reclaiming Intersectionality*

In 2013, Sumi Cho, Kimberlé Crenshaw, and Leslie McCall lead a *Signs* issue titled 'Intersectionality: Theorizing Power, Empowering Theory', which sought to consolidate the developments in intersectionality, while giving directions to future work. They were writing from within no single discipline (law, sociology, politics, literature etc.) or dimension (theory, doctrine or practice),[152] but from 'discursive spaces', that could only properly be understood as 'a burgeoning field of intersectional studies.'[153] In setting out some of the debates which had occupied the critics, the trio remarked that 'our sense is that some of what circulates as critical debate about what intersectionality is or does reflects a lack of engagement with both originating and contemporary literatures on intersectionality.'[154] This set the tone for a range of defences that sought to reclaim the ground for intersectionality by both returning to the originating context and at the same time clarifying its contemporary literatures. Much like the critiques, the defences unfolded multiply.

Sumi Cho led the charge by challenging the reductive readings of intersectionality being confined to the categories of race and sex, or Black women, as some kind of 'categorical hegemony' over the concept.[155] Her response was specifically directed towards Arriola, Valdes, Kwan and Hutchinson, who had charged intersectionality for being heteronormative in nature, and ignorant of sexuality.[156] She explained thus:

> While it is true that intersectionality's earliest applications did employ a focus on the intersection of race and gender – specifically to discuss problems of domestic violence and employment discrimination – interpreting the centering of Black women's experiences as invoking patriarchy and racism solely or exclusively is to misunderstand the Black feminism that informs intersectionality. The rootedness of intersectionality in the long intellectual and political tradition of Black feminism ensured the theory was neither heteronormative nor exclusionary.[157]

Cho also questioned the reading of intersectionality, especially in law, as too obsessed with identities and with too little regard to the structures, systems, dynamics and processes within which they were signified and became grounds

152 Cho et al. (n 21).
153 Ibid.
154 Ibid. 788.
155 Sumi Cho, 'Post-Intersectionality' (n 18).
156 Ibid. 385–387.
157 Ibid. 390.

for inequality.[158] Rita K Dhamoon similarly foregrounded what she considered central to intersectionality: a critique of power.[159] Instead, to read intersectionality literature as *not* having to do with structures especially structures of power, was seen as missing the point of intersectionality.

In Trina Grillo's 2013 review of the field, 'Anti-Essentialism and Intersectionality: Tools to Dismantle the Master's House', she pressed on the continuing significance, in fact indispensability, of the two concepts in our legal analysis. In her estimation, what is particular about intersectionality is its emphasis on wholeness of identity and subordination, such that, while identity may be co-constituted by many categories, it only makes sense when considered in its entirety. Her critique of the 'subject of the intersectional critique' was thus the inability to appreciate identities as such, and instead see them as fragmented, 'existing separately, suspended in space and time.'[160] Further, relying on a long line of literature from Arriola, Wildman and Yuval-Davis amongst others, Grillo reminded us that identities are not simply constituted along axis of subordination but are equally a matter of privilege. To see identities wholly would be to see not only those identities that are subordinated but equally, those which aren't and how both dimensions of identities together constituted the nature of discrimination for people. Intersectionality insists on the complete picture in that sense. In Grillo's succinct words, intersectionality and anti-essentialism in fact coincided in their demands asking only this: 'that we define complex experiences as closely to their full complexity as possible and that we not ignore voices at the margin.'[161]

At the same time, others like Hancock sought to systematically dismantle the ahistorical and acontextual readings of intersectionality that depoliticised its radical roots to suit more liberal aims.[162] Others like Kelly Coogan-Gehr, excavated the line of intersectional scholarship that had specifically tackled questions of class and showed that 'critiques of capitalism and imperialism have been at the heart of black feminism since its beginnings.'[163]

Sirma Bilge called out the 'whitening' of intersectionality by scholars who showed discomfort with the context and contribution of Black feminism to

158 Ibid. 393–395.
159 Rita Kaur Dhamoon, 'Considerations on Mainstreaming Intersectionality' (2011) 64 Political Research Quarterly 230.
160 Trina Grillo, 'Anti-Essentialism and Intersectionality: Tools to Dismantle the Master's House' (2013) 10 Berkley Women's Law Journal 16, 17.
161 Ibid. 22.
162 Kelly Coogan-Gehr, 'The Politics of Race in US Feminist Scholarship: An Archaeology' (2011) 37 Signs 83.
163 Ibid. 95.

the area.[164] Dismissals of Black feminist voice as 'romantic', the focus on Black women as 'too narrow', or the reliance on Black feminism as 'derivative', were thus responded with a charge of white solipsism and colonialism in feminist circles. Bilge was particularly critical of European feminists who saw race as irrelevant. Nikol Alexander-Flyod had a similar comeback to critics whose work seemed to make Black women and Black feminism disappear and dissolve in the background.[165] She went through McCall's scholarship to point out that the switch from 'subjugation' to 'complexity' in McCall's work elevated and obscured the marginalisation of Black women. This 'offstaging' of Black women and Black feminism in intersectionality literature seemed suspicious to Alexander-Flyod.[166] She was equally critical of Hancock, whose attempt to 'universalise' intersectionality as relevant to all women and operating as a general research paradigm could be classified as a 'post-Black feminist reading of intersectionality'.[167] Catharine MacKinnon too defended this reading of intersectionality: which may illuminate dynamics of privilege and subordination in a more universal sense, but its point was not that. Instead:

> Domination-and-subordination is the relational dynamic that animates this structure. It is this substantive grasp of forces that critical theories – when they are critical – are critical of, criticizing the "uncritical and disturbing acceptance of dominant ways of thinking about discrimination." Its firm grip on the way hierarchy works as a process in motion explains why this theory is not abstract, unlike the conventional equality theory of which it is critical. It is inherently substantive – hence, crucially, it does not flip. "Intersectional subordination" is a one-way ratchet, even as the analysis of it informs understanding of the status locations at both the top and the bottom of the hierarchies involved. But top and bottom are not fungible, as the classifications of race and sex are constructed to be, which explains why intersectional method could reveal the white male intersectional reality behind many challenges to affirmative action that had never before been seen or questioned as such.[168]

164 Sirma Bilge, 'Intersectionality Undone' (2013) 10 Du Bois Review 405.

165 Nikol G Alexander-Floyd, 'Disappearing Acts: Reclaiming Intersectionality in the Social Sciences in a Post-Black Feminist Era' (2012) 24 Feminist Formations 1.

166 Ibid. 12.

167 Ibid. 15.

168 Catharine A MacKinnon, 'Intersectionality as Method: A Note' (2013) 38 Signs 1019, 1024 (references omitted).

MacKinnon though has been one of the few leading "white" feminists in the US who has embraced intersectionality (though not after some criticism for having failed to do so).[169] The racial divide between intersectionalists and crits has otherwise been all too clear. Barbara Tomlinson, in her book length response to crits in 2018, sketched out the 'disturbing racial politics running through more than two decades of widely cited white feminist commentary on the intellectual property of women of colour, specifically white feminist critiques of intersectionality.'[170] For her, the critiques were 'replete with "powerblind" discursive practices that reinforce racial hierarchies and undermine feminism's stated commitment to social justice.'[171] For her, the rhetorical strategies deployed in critiquing intersectionality served as 'potent tools of dominance', trying to manage and ultimately claim power over intersectionality.[172] Because these practices almost never really *dismissed* intersectionality completely, they were seen as trying to shift its centre of control to those in power, i.e. as 'the property of a white managerial subject position'. Thus, May responded to Conaghan's critique in strong terms: 'Conaghan erases [intersectionality's] approach to subjectivity, consciousness, and power (as multiple, relational, and shifting) and instead introduces fluidity and multiplicity as her own correctives to an intersectionality weak spot.'[173] Similarly, Sora Han responded to Kwan's refinement of cosynthesis over intersectionality in these terms: 'The misrepresentation of cosynthesis as an act of critique in good faith actually leaves the reader with the sole option of moving past intersectionality without ever having encountered it. This misrepresentation subtly coerces the reader to accept second and third hand statements about intersectionality – intersectionality reduced to a 'slogan'.'[174]

Further, May explained these practices as embedded in a 'long history of minoritized groups being characterized as problems, often via an individualizing gaze that turns attention away from systems of oppression and the institutionalized social structures and cognitive norms that rationalize and maintain them.'[175] According to this view, critiques were simply interventions

169 Cf the critique of MacKinnon's work in Harris, 'Race and Essentialism' (n 77).

170 Barbara Tomlinson, *Undermining Intersectionality: The Perils of Powerblind Feminism* (Temple University Press 2018) ch 2. See also Barbara Tomlinson, 'To Tell the Truth and Not Get Trapped: Desire, Distance, and Intersectionality at the Scene of Argument' (2013) 38 Signs 993.

171 Ibid.

172 Ibid.

173 May, *Pursuing Intersectionality* (n 20) 118.

174 Sora Han, 'The Politics of Race in Asian American Jurisprudence' (2006) 11 Asian Pacific American Law Journal, 1, 30.

175 May, *Pursuing Intersectionality* (n 20) 102.

or correctives, which ended up reiterating intersectionality's main insights, from a position of power, not marginality, and thus made themselves immediately more plausible.[176] It was in this light that Crenshaw viewed much of the critique as an exercise in *disciplining*, and thus hegemonic and *against* the feminist tradition they purported to be a part of.[177]

The sum of this contemporary discourse defending intersectionality however cannot be seen as denying intersectionality's fallibilities. May admits this explicitly, that the suggestion is not that 'intersectionality is beyond debate.'[178] Rather, as she clarifies, 'the terms of critique, the forms of rhetorical containment used, the politics of plausibility in play, and the wider implications of discursive practices all "matter"'.[179] As Tomlinson recently lamented, the response to critics was really about the fact that intersectionality had become 'most misread, mischaracterized, and misunderstood'.[180] It was the process of this result that was being critiqued as much as its substance. Although, showed these responses, the substance stood vitiated in the absence of a forthright process.

Yet, neither the process nor the substance of these critiques, nor the responses to them, were seen as critical to the existence of what had already become a field of studies. Cho, Crenshaw and McCall's remark seems prescient:

> To be sure, theoretical and methodological questions will continue to mark the unfolding of intersectionality, particularly as opportunities to engage in cross-disciplinary, cross-sectoral, and international exchanges grow. Yet we do not consider the survival of or further development of intersectionality to turn on any final reconciliation of the many theoretical and methodological debates that its travel has engendered. One could look to analogous approaches to the definition of class or gender or race and realize that such debates are lively to this day and likely to never end. There are, for example, several different schools of class analysis coexisting in reasonable harmony … and the same is true with respect to race as well as gender.[181]

176 Ibid. 118.

177 Kimberlé Williams Crenshaw, 'Postscript' in Helma Lutz, Maria Teresa Herrera Vivar and Linda Supik (eds), *Framing Intersectionality: Debates on a Multi-Faceted Concept in Gender Studies* (Ashgate 2011) 223.

178 May, *Pursuing Intersectionality* (n 20) 100.

179 Ibid.

180 Tomlinson, *Undermining Intersectionality* (n 170) ch 1, 6.

181 Cho et al. (n 21) 788–789.

This is then where we seem to be at. The field of intersectionality studies emerged and evolved, is critiqued and defended, and thus continues to develop. Even the disagreements, with and within the field, seem less dangerous and more of the evidence of the vitality of the field. Another sign of vitality is its travel through comparative antidiscrimination law, and beyond antidiscrimination law in the US. How far has intersectionality penetrated this context? That is, from when Crenshaw posited her initial critique, how far has intersectionality come in antidiscrimination law, and does its rich and long trajectory of development bear out in the developments across jurisdictions? The next part steers the discussion towards these inquires.

## Part 3: Comparative Antidiscrimination Law

The trajectory of intersectionality theory is long, considerable and formidable. The developments in intersectionality have been significant in broadening our socio-political understanding of people's experiences of discrimination, and to an extent, in highlighting how intersectional discrimination falls through the cracks of antidiscrimination law. The discussion in this part makes it apparent that law, especially antidiscrimination law, has been a recurrent theme in the story of development of intersectionality. It is then useful to measure the depth of intersectionality's engagement with antidiscrimination law, and whether the initial critique – of intersectionality falling through the cracks – continues to hold, or whether like the developments in intersectionality, antidiscrimination law too has come of age. It is particularly useful to see this in a comparative context, because intersectional concerns seemed to have proliferated everywhere and beyond its initial site: the US. What comes through in the two sections that follow is that while comparative antidiscrimination law seems to have developed with intersectionality in sight, it has never quite developed with intersectionality in step. What that means is that intersectionality has been present and engaged with but never quite translated into mainstream antidiscrimination law. On the other hand, the scholarship that has engaged with the comparative judicial doctrine has been more promising, and has consistently and substantively engaged with intersectionality, including like Crenshaw, continuing to critique antidiscrimination law's resistance to intersectionality.

### 3.1 *Judicial Doctrine and Intersectionality*

The judicial doctrine from four jurisdictions (US, UK, Canada and South Africa) reveals antidiscrimination law's long-held resistance towards intersectionality.

But what it also reveals is that the resistance seems to have coexisted with frequent nods and lip service paid to intersectionality. While the latter, prominent in Canada and South Africa, is itself somewhat of a progress, it by no means matches the developmental strides made by intersectionality outside of the antidiscrimination discourse. It is the substance of the judicial doctrine that shows this divergence most distinctly.

### 3.1.1 US

Crenshaw's first conceptualisation of intersectionality sought to explicate how race and gender both affected Black women's employment experiences and in trying to subsume their experience in either the race or the gender discourse, antidiscrimination law failed to appreciate those at the intersections of both. This discussion was informed by her analysis in three cases before the American courts: *DeGraffenreid v General Motors*,[182] *Payne v Trevanol*[183] and *Moore v Hughes*.[184] The first of these – *DeGraffenreid* – remains the gold standard of intersectional flop. This case was at the centre of Crenshaw's critique and the 1989 piece that led to the christening of intersectionality.

The plaintiffs in *DeGraffenreid* sought a determination that the General Motors' 'last hired-first fired' lay off policy discriminated against them as Black women.[185] The United States District Court of Missouri summarily dismissed the possibility that claims could be based on a combination of grounds (race and sex) and hence plaintiffs were denied the right to claim as Black women who suffered both race and sex discrimination. It interpreted the synergistic nature of the claim as a demand for recognising a 'new special sub-category'[186] or 'special class'[187] for the grant of a 'new "super-remedy"'[188] beyond the contours of Title VII of the Civil Rights Act of 1964 which prohibits discrimination on the basis of race, colour, religion, sex or national origin. According to the Court, the 'lawsuit must be examined to see if it states a cause of action for race discrimination, sex discrimination, or alternatively either, but not a combination of both.'[189] Thus, Black women could be protected only to the extent that their experience coincided either with that of Black men or white women. However, neither Black men nor white women provided an apposite

---

182 413 F Supp 142 (ED Mo 1976).
183 673 F 2d 798 (5th Cir 1982).
184 708 F 2d 475 (9th Cir 1983).
185 *DeGraffenreid* (n 182) 143.
186 Ibid. 143.
187 Ibid.
188 Ibid.
189 Ibid.

comparator group since the statistical evidence indicated that both groups were hired and retained by General Motors. They were thus *not* fired under this policy. It was the absence of discrimination against Black men and white women that should have alerted the Court to the uniqueness of Black women's compounded claim. Instead, the Court understood the claim as neither about race or sex discrimination, nor about the combination of both, but as a request for inclusion of a new ground for 'a new classification of "black women"', and thus opening the 'the hackneyed Pandora's box' for the creation of new classes of protected minorities under Title VII.[190]

Four years later, the Fifth Circuit Federal Court of Appeal *in Jefferies v Harris County Community Action*[191] accepted that Black women could be discriminated against even in the absence of discrimination against Black men and white women and recognised them as a distinct subgroup protected under Title VII.[192] But the gains made in *Jefferies* were limited six years later in *Judge v Marsh*.[193] According to the Court:

> The difficulty with [the *Jefferies*'] position is that it turns employment discrimination into a many-headed Hydra, impossible to contain within Title VII's prohibition. Following the *Jeffries* rationale to its extreme, protected subgroups would exist for every possible combination of race, color, sex, national origin and religion ... For this reason, the *Jeffries* analysis is appropriately limited to employment decisions based on one protected, immutable trait or fundamental right, which are directed against individuals sharing a second protected, immutable characteristic ... The benefits of Title VII thus will not be splintered beyond use and recognition; nor will they be constricted and unable to reach discrimination based on the existing unlawful criteria.[194]

The fear expressed in *Judge* has since limited the number of relevant grounds in a discrimination claim to two. Thus, the cases that now seem to succeed are all argued on two grounds, both of which are explicitly recognised under

190 Ibid. 145.

191 *Jefferies v Harris County Community Action Assn*, 615 F 2d 1025 (5th Cir 1980) (US Federal Court of Appeals).

192 Ibid. 1034. Followed in *Lam v University of Hawaii* 40 F 3d 1551 (9th Cir 1994); *Chambers v Omaha Girls Club* 629 F Supp 925, 942 (D Neb 1986); *Graham v Bendix Corp* 585 F Supp 1036, 1047 (ND Ind 1984).

193 *Judge v Marsh* 649 F Supp 770 (1986) 779.

194 Ibid. 780.

Title VII, and with respect to a specific class, viz. minority women;[195] while the possibility of arguing as a different class, or on an analogous ground, or arguing on grounds under two different statutes, remain bleak. It is useful to illustrate these scenarios.

In the first instance, it appears that while Black women are now admitted as a class, the possibility of extending a claim based on two grounds to other classes seems to evade. Thus, Black women seem to find it difficult to claim on behalf of Black men[196] or white women.[197] Black women really seem to be a category of their own, and not representative of 'pure' race or sex discrimination. Although successful plaintiffs have not only been Black women, but women of colour and minority women in general. Thus, in the most celebrated case of *Lam v University of Hawaii*, the Court found in favour of a woman of Vietnamese descent. She had claimed discrimination on the basis of race, sex and national origin in hiring for the position of Director of the University of Hawaii Law School's Pacific Asian Legal Studies Program. She was disparaged, her abilities undermined, especially in comparison to two other candidates, one Asian man and a white woman. Despite, the Court found that it wasn't the presence of favourable treatment of comparators, but the treatment of the plaintiff itself that justified her claim. It asserted, that even 'favorable treatment of other Asian women would not necessarily defeat Lam's claim at trial.'[198] It explained the nature of the claim thus:

> where two bases for discrimination exist, they cannot be neatly reduced to distinct components … Rather than aiding the decisional process, the attempt to bisect a person's identity at the intersection of race and gender often distorts or ignores the particular nature of their experiences … Like other subclasses under Title VII, Asian women are subject to a set of stereotypes and assumptions shared neither by Asian men nor by white women. In consequence, they may be targeted for discrimination "even in the absence of discrimination against [Asian] men or white women." … Accordingly, we agree with the Jefferies court that, when a plaintiff is claiming race and sex bias, it is necessary to determine whether the employer discriminates on the basis of that combination of factors,

195 For example, *Hicks v Gates Rubber Co* 833 F 2d 1406 (10th Cir 1987); *Lam* (n 192); *Goodwin v Board of Trustees of University of Illinois* 442 F 3d 611 (7th Cir 2006); *Shazor v Professional Transit Management Ltd* 744 F 3d 948 (6th Cir 2014); *Kimble v Wisconsin Department of Workforce Dev* 690 F Supp 2d 765.

196 *Lewis v Bloomsburg Mills, Inc* 773 F 2d 561 (4th Cir 1985).

197 *Moore v Hughes* 708 F 2d 475 (9th Cir 1983).

198 *Lam* (n 192) 1561.

> not just whether it discriminates against people of the same race or of the same sex.[199]

*Lam* provided the real breakthrough in US jurisprudence. It dismantled the idea that a claim based on two grounds needed to be evaluated independently in any way. The only construction of that claim was compounded, with evidence that went towards both grounds simultaneously.[200] Two years later, *Church's* repeated this line of reasoning:

> a defendant cannot rebut a *prima facia* case of intentional discrimination against a black female by showing that female employees as a whole were treated the same as all males employees or that black employees as a whole were treated the same as white employees. The purpose is to focus specifically on the treatment of black females as compared to every other employee outside the class of black females.[201]

Yet, it is important to note that the final proof was still based on comparative evidence and *Church*'s eventually failed in the absence of it. In the final analysis, the claim was declined because the Court found that the claimant had not 'provided a meaningful comparison of her salary with those of managers outside her class of black females, namely white males, white females, and black males.'[202] The result is that, while claims by minority women are now accepted in principle, they continue to be hard to establish. The courts seem to accept the premise of intersectionality and yet continue to evaluate it on the basis of grounds individually. The result resembles multiple discrimination instead of intersectional discrimination, when multiple grounds are examined for their discriminatory effect independently rather than for their intersectional impact. Take for example the case of *Jeffers v Thompson*,[203] where the court declared in succession:

> to apply Title VII as written when a plaintiff claims race-and-gender bias, the court must determine "whether the employer discriminates on the basis of that combination of factors, not just whether it discriminates against people of the same race or the same sex." ... Relevant – though

---

199 Ibid. 1562 (references omitted).

200 See though a possible critique of *Lam* in Atrey, *Intersectional Discrimination* (n 2) 116–117.

201 *Daniels v Church's Chicken* 942 F Supp 533 (1996) 538.

202 Ibid.

203 (2003) 264 F Supp 2d 314, 326 (D Md 2003).

> not dispositive – evidence of such a claim includes evidence of discrimination against African-Americans (regardless of gender) and evidence of discrimination against females (regardless of race).[204]
>
> HHS [the defendant] promoted a 44yearold Caucasian male and a 50yearold Caucasian female instead of Ms. Jeffers. Because one of the applicants selected was a woman, and because no other evidence of pure gender discrimination has been adduced, Ms. Jeffers has failed to establish a *prima facie* case of pure gender discrimination ... She has, however, established a prima facie case of composite, race-and-gender discrimination because HHS did not promote an African-American woman ... [But the] sparse statistical evidence discloses no special bias against African-American women. From the totality of the evidence, no rational factfinder could conclude that HHS failed to promote Ms. Jeffers because of the combination of her race-and-gender.[205]

Similar analysis ensued in *Jeffers* with respect to age, where the court was not convinced that there was sufficient evidence that age in particular played a role in a race-and-gender claim or independently. In fact, it appears that when age is involved at all, courts are generally slow in treating evidence cumulatively and look for independent evidence that goes towards 'pure' age discrimination to be later combined with other evidence in a multi-ground claim.[206] This selective treatment of evidence to establish grounds separately seems to indicate that the courts struggle with the logic of intersectionality not conceptually, at least not any longer, but operationally. They *get* that intersectional claims cannot be so neatly separated but do not quite follow this cue when it comes to proof.

Finally, in the second instance, it is useful to note that the claims are often confined to two grounds already listed in Title VII and that claims are rarely, if ever, based on analogous grounds, or based on grounds across legislations. Thus, claims combining causes of action under Title VII grounds (race, colour, sex, religion, national origin) and under, say, the American Disabilities Act, seldom succeed as a whole. For example, in a case like *Lowe v Angelo's Italian Foods, Inc*,[207] the plaintiff's disability claim was allowed to succeed while her race claim was shelved. The evidence was disparate in nature. At various

204 Ibid. 327.

205 Ibid. 327.

206 *Hill v Lockheed Martin Logistics Mgmt., Inc* 354 F 3d 277, 283 (4th Cir 2004); *Gorzynski v JetBlue Airways Corp.* 596 F 3d 93, 110 (2d Cir 2010).

207 87 F 3d 1170 (10th Cir 1996).

instances, the plaintiff was mistreated at the workplace, called names in racially and sexually explicit terms, and fired when she requested disability-related leave of absence. Very similar facts existed in *Joseph v HDMJ Restaurant, Inc*,[208] though the Court allowed the race and not the disability claim to proceed.[209] When more than two grounds are involved, such as in *Chaddah v Harris Bank Glencoe-Northbrook, NA*,[210] which concerned a plaintiff's case as an older Asian woman, the Court could not find a way to proceed on either age, race or gender, or a combination of some.

The record of the US courts thus appears patchy. In MacKinnon's words, the US experience with intersectionality oscillates between truly getting it, and truly missing it.[211] The courts seemed to have grasped the intersectional logic in the case of minority women and missed it in other contexts. Thus, while intersectional scholarship seems to have responded to these debates – of limiting intersectionality to single-axis, to two grounds, to race and sex, and to the category of Black women or minority women – it seems that the courts are still mired in them. The developments in intersectionality theory in the US and the position of US courts after thirty years of Crenshaw's reigning critique thus seem to be at very different points of evolution: the former clearly having surpassed the latter, and the latter remaining the subject of critique of the former as ever.

### 3.1.2 UK

The UK Equality Act 2010 specifically includes a provision titled 'combined discrimination' based on 'dual characteristics'. It provides in part:

> 14 Combined discrimination: dual characteristics
>
> (1) A person (A) discriminates against another (B) if, because of a combination of two relevant protected characteristics, A treats B less favourably than A treats or would treat a person who does not share either of those characteristics.
>
> (2) The relevant protected characteristics are –
>
> (a) age;
>
> (b) disability;
>
> (c) gender reassignment;

---

208 970 F Supp 2d 131 (EDNY 2013).

209 See also *Accord Herx v Diocese of Fort Wayne-S Bend, Inc* 772 F 3d 1085 (7th Cir 2014); *Querry v Messar* 14 F Supp 2d 437 (SDNY 1998).

210 42 F 3d 1391 (7th Cir 1994).

211 MacKinnon (n 168) 1022.

(d) race;
(e) religion or belief;
(f) sex;
(g) sexual orientation.
(3) For the purposes of establishing a contravention of this Act by virtue of subsection (1), B need not show that A's treatment of B is direct discrimination because of each of the characteristics in the combination (taken separately).

Section 14 is thus limited to a set of grounds, and excludes other grounds like marital status and pregnancy, otherwise recognised in the Equality Act. It is also limited to cases of direct discrimination. The provision was initially slated to come into force in 2011, but has actually never been brought into effect. Thus, despite its obvious shortcomings, it has never been tested against intersectionality anyway. It remains to be seen whether Section 14 could potentially accommodate intersectionality. Until then, the precedent for claiming intersectionality remains a case that maps onto the result in *DeGraffenreid* squarely. *Bahl v Law Society*[212] mirrors *DeGraffenreid* in that the claim based on two grounds is split into independent claims to be proven separately. The difference between the two claims is that while the *DeGraffenreid* Court insisted that the claimant could only argue on a single ground and so must choose between race and sex, the *Bahl* Court allowed the claimant to argue on two grounds but prove them separately. Yet again, the *Bahl* reasoning signifies an understanding better described as multiple rather than intersectional discrimination and matches much of the US jurisprudence which continues to treat intersectional cases as multiple discrimination.

In *Bahl*, the UK Court of Appeal was dealing with a challenge to unfair dismissal on grounds of race and sex by the appellant, Dr Kamlesh Bahl, who was a Black Asian woman. Dr Bahl was the Vice President of the Law Society and alleged that she had been discriminated against by its members, especially its President and Secretary General in the determination of staff complaints against her behaviour. In analysing the copious evidence presented before the courts below, Peter Gibson LJ at the Court of Appeal found that the Employment Tribunal had omitted to 'identify what evidence goes to support a finding of race discrimination and what evidence goes to support a finding of sex discrimination' and that it would have been 'surprising if the evidence for each form of discrimination was the same.'[213] He insisted that for a claim

212 *Bahl v Law Society* [2004] EWCA Civ 1070 (UK Court of Appeal).
213 Ibid. [137].

of race and sex discrimination to succeed the claimant should be able to prove both sex and race discrimination *separately* such that discrimination was based on 'either race or sex'.[214] This route to examining a multi-ground claim may have resulted from the atomised nature of the UK discrimination law at the time where sex was a protected ground under the Sex Discrimination Act 1975 and racial discrimination was prohibited separately under the Race Relations Act 1976. But aside from this technicality, it is difficult to agree with the Court of Appeal's final ruling dismissing Dr Bahl's appeal by treating her claim as one of multiple rather than intersectional discrimination. In multiple discrimination, each ground is taken in turn and churned through the discrimination inquiry one after the other to establish discrimination. It thus represents nothing more than multiple single-ground claims treated successively.

Having decided that the claim was to be examined as a matter of multiple discrimination, the Court employed the comparator test to assist its discrimination inquiry. It asked the claimant to show how her disadvantage as a Black woman was so unique and different from a white man.[215] This approach obscures the nature of discrimination yielded by the intersection of dual grounds. First, by pitching the 'uniqueness' of the claim so high and distant by comparing the claimant's experience with a white male, the Court is unable to appreciate the distinctive disadvantage accruing to the claimant as a Black woman on its own terms. The standard against which the claimant is measured is so removed from her own claim that the purpose of understanding the unique disadvantage as suffered by *her* transmogrifies into comparison with an unrelated standard. Secondly, the Court also debars any 'shared' patterns of disadvantage based on race and sex. That the claimant's experiences of racism and sexism may potentially coincide with that of Black men and white women respectively was left unexamined.[216] The fact that mirror comparison here required comparison with those similarly situated as the claimant, and not any other Black women, Black men or white women, made it impossible to refer to comparable experiences within the organisation albeit at a different 'level' than the claimant. Thirdly, the approach undermines the claimant's identity by insisting on treating disadvantage flowing from different aspects of her identity in a fragmented way. In fact, the Court specifically rejects the Employment Tribunal's approach, which had refused to isolate the sexist and

214 Ibid. [115]–[137].

215 *Bahl* (n 212) [103].

216 Aileen McColgan, 'Reconfiguring Discrimination Law' [2007] Public Law 74, 81.

racist aspects of alleged discrimination, calling this approach 'puzzling' and erroneous.[217] The Employment Tribunal had found that:

> We do not distinguish between the race or sex of the Applicant in reaching this conclusion. Our reason for that is simple. The claim was advanced on the basis that Kamlesh Bahl was treated in the way she was *because she is a black woman*. Kamlesh Bahl was the first office holder that the Law Society had ever had who was not both white and male. There was no basis in the evidence for comparing her treatment with that of a white female, or a black male, office holder. We can only draw inferences ... It is sufficient for our purposes to find, where appropriate, that in each case they would not have treated a white person or a man less favourably.[218]

Besides what the Court of Appeal was actually saying in *Bahl*, it is interesting to note what it was doing in fact. The Court of Appeal maintained a constant focus on 'the reason why',[219] for finding an explanation for the detrimental treatment and whether the conduct was motivated by 'discriminatory reasons'.[220] The consideration of evidence was lengthy and thorough in deciphering any discriminatory treatment and its basis. The Court thus remarked: 'A charge of discrimination is a very serious matter to find established against anyone, let alone the President and the Secretary General of the Law Society. Fairness demanded that the finding of discrimination be adequately explained and shown to have a proper evidential basis.'[221] This focus on the reason why discrimination occurred is right – while the intensive set of facts in this case failed to reveal the basis of discriminatory treatment in race and sex, it is arguable that a case with a more sympathetic claimant would have been licit. And if a court does not insist on answering the 'why' question in a splintered way (as the *Bahl* Court seem to suggest), it may even find discriminatory reasons to be causally linked to multiple grounds in a synergistic way.[222]

---

217 *Bahl* (n 212) [136]–[137].

218 Ibid. [135] (emphasis supplied).

219 Ibid. [126]; *Shamoon v Chief Constable of the Royal Ulster Constabulary* [2003] UKHL 11 [7]–[10].

220 Ibid. [101], [134], [147].

221 Ibid. [134].

222 It is useful to note again that discriminatory reasons in cases of direct intersectional discrimination do not necessarily mean the presence of animus, motive or intention to discriminate. So long as discriminatory effects or impact *flow from* or are *based on* multiple grounds in some way, the discrimination inquiry should be satisfied in its search for the reason why discrimination occurred. See Tarunabh Khaitan, *A Theory of Discrimination*

This seems to be the line pursued in Section 14 of the Equality Act, which provides that it is not necessary to show that the treatment complained of was direct discrimination 'because of each of the characteristics in the combination (taken separately).' If Section 14 were brought into effect, the *Bahl* approach would lose ground. While Section 14 remains unenforced, the prevailing law on direct and indirect discrimination under Sections 13 and 19 respectively may continue to tread the line in *Bahl*, since they relate only to single-axis discrimination. A court may decide a multi-ground claim by churning it through single-axis analysis in Section 13 or 19 multiple times, thus yielding multiple rather than intersectional discrimination. Thus, as Fredman remarks: 'although [Equality Act] is an important breakthrough, it remains the case that the more a person differs from the norm [single-axis discrimination], the less likely she is to gain protection.'[223]

There are glimmers of hope, however. Despite an unenforced Section 14 and the position in *Bahl*, intersectionality seems to have been covertly, almost disconcertingly quietly, accepted by the Supreme Court in its 2012 decision – *Hewage v Grampian Health Board*.[224] The claimant, a British Asian woman, worked as an orthodontist for the Grampian Health Board. She complained of unfair dismissal under the Employment Rights Act 1996 and discrimination on the basis of sex and race under the Sex Discrimination Act 1975 and the Race Relations Act 1976 respectively. She argued that 'other white male consultants were not subjected to the same bullying and harassing treatment'.[225] The Supreme Court was specifically asked to examine the validity of the choice of the white male comparator offered as proof of discriminatory treatment. Without much ado about the fact that the claim devolved on two grounds and was thus potentially a case of intersectionality, the Supreme Court approved the choice of comparison and thereby confirmed the possibility of claiming discrimination on two grounds without having to argue each separately. *Hewage* thus seemed to have modified the *Bahl* ratio wherein a white male comparator was deemed acceptable only to prove race *or* sex discrimination but not *both*. The latter is now possible under *Hewage*.

It seems that the *Hewage* approach actually only confirms what the tribunals in the UK have been doing anyway. In fact, the tribunals have seemed to do intersectionality despite the disappointing result in *Bahl* and the corrective

---

*Law* (OUP 2015) 165–171. Cf John Gardner, 'On the Ground of Her Sex(uality)' (1998) 18 Oxford Journal of Legal Studies 167.

223 Sandra Fredman, *Discrimination Law* (2nd edn, OUP 2011) 143.

224 2012 IRLR 870 SC.

225 Ibid. [12].

offered in *Hewage*.[226] Dame Laura Cox's opinion in *Tilern de Bique* is particularly noteworthy because despite all the restrictions that exist in the UK law, the opinion is salient in its intersectional analysis. The case before the Employment Appeal Tribunal concerned a Foreign and Commonwealth soldier serving in the British Army, who was a single mother with a young daughter. She alleged that the Ministry of Defence had indirectly discriminated against her on the basis of race and sex by imposing conditions that affected her as a non-British soldier and single mother. The conditions included a 24×7 requirement for soldiers to be available at all times, irrespective of their gender or child-care status. In order for soldiers to meet this requirement, they were encouraged to seek help from family members for childcare. But non-British family members were not allowed to immigrate to provide for childcare under the immigration law. The claimant was unable to meet the 24×7 condition because she could not seek her family's help with childcare as a non-British national. She compared her treatment to other soldiers who were men and would not commonly have been in the same position as fathers with full-time primary childcare. She also compared her treatment to other single mothers, who, if they were British nationals, would have been able to access childcare. While the claimant's own sister was willing to provide assistance, because she was Caribbean and not British, was unable to obtain a visa for this purpose. The claimant was thus uniquely compromised by the operation of the 24×7 and the immigration conditions. Approving the Tribunal's finding in favour of the claimant, Dame Cox explained thus:

> In general, the nature of discrimination is such that it cannot always be sensibly compartmentalised into discrete categories. Whilst some complainants will raise issues relating to only one or other of the prohibited grounds, attempts to view others as raising only one form of discrimination for consideration will result in an inadequate understanding and assessment of the complainant's true disadvantage. Discrimination is often a multi-faceted experience. The Claimant in this case considered that the particular disadvantage to which she was subject arose both because she was a 24/7 female soldier with a child and because she was a woman of Vincentian national origin, for whom childcare assistance from a live-in Vincentian relative was not permitted. The Tribunal recognised that this, double disadvantage reflected the factual reality of her situation.[227]

226 *O'Reilly v BBC* [2010] UKET/2200423/2010; *Ministry of Defence v Tilern De Bique* [2009] UKEAT/0075/11/SM.

227 *Tilern* ibid. [165].

The recognition of the multi-faceted experience of discrimination in *Tilern* is an important contribution to the recognition of intersectionality at the tribunal level. It goes far beyond the apparent statutory limitations of restricting combination of grounds to race and sex, and looks into child-care status and nationality as aspects of racial and sexual subordination of someone in the position of the claimant. It showed particular awareness of the context of military service and its national and masculine overtones. It went beyond tracing intersectionality in direct discrimination alone and was keen in its observation of indirect patterns of disadvantage associated with race and sex both. It did not fragment the identity of the claimant at any point and showed how the judicial narrative could positively affirm and respect the identity of intersectional claimants. Thus, despite what seems to be the authoritative position in the UK – the unenforced Section 14 and a piecemeal acceptance of intersectionality in *Hewage* – the tribunals seem to have charted their own course to intersectionality in a promising way.

### 3.1.3 Canada

Section 15(1) of the Canadian Charter of Rights and Freedoms ('Canadian Charter') provides for equality before and under law and equal protection and benefit of law as follows: 'Every individual is equal before and under the law and has the right to the equal protection and equal benefit of the law without discrimination and, in particular, without discrimination based on race, national or ethnic origin, colour, religion, sex, age or mental or physical disability.'

The text of sub-section (1) does not expressly recognise the possibility of bringing a discrimination claim on more than one ground, but there is nothing in the general guarantee of the 'right to the equal protection and equal benefit of the law without discrimination' which debars such a claim either. That said, the Canadian Supreme Court has never decided an intersectional claim. Given this record, it is interesting to analyse cases that were considered to be intersectional cases in fact. This array of cases is substantial. The theme that emerges from it is the constant jostling with multiple grounds to determine which *one* caused discrimination as such. This is despite the Supreme Court's frequent admission that discrimination *could* be based on multiple grounds that cannot neatly be separated from one another. Yet, the actual analysis of claims that could potentially have been decided as intersectional claims seems to indicate a resistance to this view in practice.

*Mossop v Canada*[228] is one of the earliest cases that shows the Canadian Supreme Court's insistence on a single-axis framework. In *Mossop*, the

228 *Mossop v Canada (Attorney General)* [1993] 1 SCR 554.

claimant alleged discrimination for being denied bereavement leave to attend the funeral of his partner's father. The bereavement leave was denied since the claimant's same-sex relationship with his partner was not recognised within the impugned provision concerning the 'immediate family' of a 'common law spouse'. At the first instance, the claimant challenged the denial of bereavement leave under sections 7(b), 9(1)(c) and 10(b) of the Canadian Human Rights Act (CHRA) for being discriminatory on the ground of 'family status'.[229] The issue whether family status included same-sex individuals came to be considered before the Canadian Supreme Court. According to the Court, the matter could have been decided on the ground of sexual orientation if it was pleaded as such and in particular, if it constituted a ground under the CHRA.[230] But instead, the claimant had chosen the ground of family status under the CHRA. That, however, was not the ground of discrimination because, according to Lamer CJ:

> It is sexual orientation which has led the complainant to enter with [his partner] into a "familial relationship" (to use the expression of the expert sociologist) and sexual orientation, therefore, which has precluded the recognition of his family status with regard to his lover and that man's father. So in final analysis, sexual orientation is *really the ground of discrimination* involved.[231]

This reasoning demonstrates a narrow understanding of both 'grounds' as well as 'discrimination'. First, when a ground like sexual orientation is not enumerated, it becomes difficult to have it recognised as an analogous ground even in an open-ended list of grounds. But because it *is* deemed to be the ground of discrimination in fact, it becomes impossible for the claimant to succeed on another relevant ground like marital status. The irony is obvious: while sexual orientation was deemed to be the ground of discrimination, it was not a 'ground' of discrimination legislatively. Second, the presence of multiple grounds seems to embroil the Court in delineating which of them is '*really* the ground of discrimination involved'.[232] In *Mossop*, Lamer CJ jostles with 'sexual orientation' and 'family status' to pin down *one* of these as bearing on the

229 Canadian Human Rights Act, R.S.C., 1985, c. H-6 ('3. (1) For all purposes of this Act, race, national or ethnic origin, colour, religion, age, sex, marital status, family status, disability and conviction for which a pardon has been granted are prohibited grounds of discrimination.').

230 *Mossop* (n 228) 31–32.

231 Ibid. 33 (emphasis supplied).

232 Ibid. 33 (emphasis supplied).

discrimination inquiry, rather than focussing on analysing their interrelationship. The approach seems to arise from an unnecessary and incomprehensible logic of single-axis discrimination. In her dissent, L'Heureux-Dubé J instead decried this idea and instead acknowledged the possibility of intersectional discrimination:

> It is increasingly recognized that categories of discrimination may overlap, and that individuals may suffer historical exclusion on the basis of both race and gender, age and physical handicap, or some other combination. The situation of individuals who confront multiple grounds of disadvantage is particularly complex … Categorizing such discrimination as primarily racially oriented, or primarily gender-oriented, misconceives the reality of discrimination as it is experienced by individuals. Discrimination may be experienced on many grounds, and where this is the case, it is not really meaningful to assert that it is one or the other. It may be more realistic to recognize that both forms of discrimination may be present and intersect. On a practical level, where both forms of discrimination are prohibited, one can ignore the complexity of the interaction, and characterize the discrimination as of one type or the other. The person is protected from discrimination in either event.[233]
>
> When faced with such situations, one should be cautious not to characterize the discrimination so as to deprive the person of any protection … One should not lightly allow a characterization which excludes those from the scope of the Act who should legitimately be included. A narrow and exclusionary approach, in my view, is inconsistent with a broad and purposive interpretation of human rights legislation.[234]

Despite L'Heureux-Dubé J's credible dissent cautioning against narrow, exclusionary and categorical approaches to discrimination, the majority in *Mossop* was consumed by the single-axis view of both grounds as well as discrimination. This trend though appears to have been fortified in later case law.

*Mossop* was soon followed by *Egan v Canada*.[235] It concerned the provisions of the Old Age Security Act (OASA) that provided for an allowance to spouses of pensioners whose income fell below a stipulated amount, when they reached the age of 60 and until they became pensioners at 65. The claimants alleged that the impugned welfare provisions discriminated against persons living in

233 Ibid. 106.

234 Ibid. 107.

235 *Egan v Canada* [1995] 2 SCR 513.

a homosexual relationship because the legislation restricted the definition of 'spouse' to individuals in a heterosexual union, i.e. those who were legally married or were in a common law relationship. The claimants challenged this to be in violation of Section 15 of the Canadian Charter on the ground of sexual orientation.[236] The majority accepted that sexual orientation constituted an analogous ground of discrimination under section 15,[237] but did not consider that the distinction under the OASA constituted discrimination for the purposes of the Canadian Charter. In reaching this conclusion, the Court considered the distinction made by the Parliament that depended upon 'the nature of the personal characteristic and its relevancy to the functional values underlying the law.'[238] According to La Forest J, the relevancy of the distinction was one 'both obvious and deeply rooted in our fundamental values and traditions, values and traditions that could not have been lost on the framers of the Charter. Simply stated, what Parliament clearly had in mind was to accord support to married couples who were aged and elderly, and this for the advancement of public policy central to society.'[239] In preserving the 'fundamental importance of marriage as a social institution',[240] the majority did not seek to interrogate the discriminatory aspects of the 'biological and social realities of marriage', which it accepted as such without more.[241] The Court found that homosexual couples were excluded just as other 'couples living together' were, including brothers, sisters, relatives and un-related persons, regardless of their sex or sexual orientation.[242] There was little appreciation of the fact that none of other said relationships were *excluded* and *disadvantaged* by the denial of access to an institution like marriage. The lack of engagement with the reality of the lives of James Egan and John Norris Nesbit as a homosexual couple, who were both aged and in need of income supplement, seems to have resulted from a disengaged reading of their identities, where sexual orientation, marital status, age or class seemed to have little to do with one another.

And yet, in actuality, all of these fused together to yield the disadvantage experienced by the claimants. This was recognised in L'Heureux-Dubé J's dissent, which understood discrimination in light of 'real people's real experiences'[243] by focussing on the impact (i.e. discriminatory effect) rather than the basis

236 Ibid. [5].
237 Ibid.
238 Ibid. 28–29 (quoting Gonthier J in *Miron v Trudel* [1995] 2 SCR 418, 436).
239 Ibid. [20].
240 Ibid. [21].
241 Ibid. [27].
242 Ibid. [19].
243 Ibid. [53].

of discrimination (i.e. the grounds).[244] L'Heureux-Dubé J considered grounds to be 'an imperfect vehicle'[245] that skewed the inquiry towards the question: 'whether the characteristics *of the ground* are sufficient to constitute a basis for discrimination, rather than into the absence or presence of discriminatory *effects* themselves.'[246] Her dissenting opinion thus concentrated on finding the effects, through a multi-layered focus on the nature of interest affected, the socio-economic disadvantage, and the stereotypes and prejudice associated with the exclusion under the OASA. L'Heureux-Dubé J did not analyse the effects as flowing from the claimant's identities or grounds of discrimination, i.e. age, class, marital status and sexual orientation, but instead saw these identities as simply bearing out in the context of discrimination which was about the affective reality of such discrimination rather than abstract categories or 'grounds'. According to her, the 'enumerated or analogous nature of a given ground should not be a necessary precondition to a finding of discrimination.'[247] Instead, she suggested that:

> Given the growing reliance on "context", and the declining role of the "grounds of distinction", I believe that it is a natural next step in s. 15 jurisprudence to admit that, in fact, context is of primary importance and that abstract "grounds of distinction" are simply an indirect method to achieve a goal which could be achieved more simply and truthfully by asking the direct question: "Does this distinction discriminate against this group of people?"[248]

That said, even the majority had avowed to apply a 'comprehensive contextual approach'[249] in assessing the claim. They however had not abandoned looking for the ground or the basis of discrimination. Context seems to be invoked in very different ways then by the majority and the minority. However, context has never come to replace grounds as such, despite L'Heureux-Dubé J's suggestion in *Egan*. The jurisprudence of the Supreme Court of Canada continues to be in line with the majority approach in *Mossop* and *Egan*, of always linking discrimination to grounds, even if, in context. Thus, later case law, especially

244 Ibid. [39].
245 Ibid. 44.
246 Ibid. [47] (emphasis in original).
247 Ibid. [52].
248 Ibid. [82].
249 Ibid. [18] [25] (La Forest J), [82] (L'Heureux-Dubé J, dissenting).

*Law v Canada*[250] and *R v Kapp*[251] have both retained grounds as the threshold requirement for invoking discrimination, while also involving 'contextual factors' in the determination of discrimination. The four enumerated 'contextual factors' in *Law* included: pre-existing disadvantage; correspondence between the ground of distinction and the actual needs and circumstances of the affected group; the ameliorative purpose or effect of the impugned measure for a more disadvantaged group; and the nature and scope of the interests affected. This approach to the discrimination analysis alludes to a holistic discrimination inquiry by analysing a range of circumstances surrounding the claim, claimant and the impugned legislation. Yet, it does not quite help solve the hurdle of single-axis discrimination where discrimination is embedded in a single ground and never really on multiple grounds. If it does leave open the possibility for discrimination to be based on multiple grounds, accounted as either 'grounds' or 'context' of the claim, it is not clear how that analysis would be carried out to reflect intersectionality. Just as the approach does not seem to have worked in *Egan*, it does not seem to have worked for other complex cases of discrimination either.[252] But if not this, at least two other things seem to have worked. First, intersectionality, where explicitly addressed in a legislation, has been protected from discrimination by courts. Second, intersectionality seems to have been recognised via embedded grounds.

*Law v Canada* is a good example of the first. *Law* was an age discrimination claim against a statutory pension provision reducing the pension for non-disabled surviving spouses who were between the ages of 35–45 years and were without dependent children, by 1/120th of the full rate. This was challenged as age discrimination under the Canadian Charter. The Supreme Court agreed with the government's view that the distinction was not solely based on age but rather 'a combination of age, healthful employability, and freedom from the responsibility of dependent children'.[253] The fact that discrimination, if any, was *not* single-axis, was thus seen as not giving rise to discrimination at all, though the Court was open to the argument that discrimination based on multiple grounds could be potentially discriminatory.[254] But the *Law* carve-out

250 *Law v Canada* [1999] 1 SCR 497.

251 *R v Kapp* [2008] 2 SCR 483.

252 See *Gosselin v Quebec (Attorney General)* [2002] 4 SCR 429.

253 Ibid. [15].

254 Ibid. [94] ('There is no reason in principle, therefore, why a discrimination claim positing an intersection of grounds cannot be understood as analogous to, or as a synthesis of, the grounds listed in s. 15(1). In the present case, if the CPP had based entitlement on a combination of factors, the appellant would still have been able to establish the requisite distinction, whether on the basis of age alone, or based on a combination of grounds.').

survived because it was intended to exclude more privileged persons whilst trying to include those who were multiply disadvantaged, by their disability, age and child-care status, for higher pension. The intersectional carve-out thus helped save the beneficial provision in *Law*. However, it is clear that unlike *Law*, when intersectional claimants are not protected explicitly, such as in *Mossop* and *Egan*, discrimination is hard to be established.

*Corbiere* is a good example of the second instance where intersectional discrimination succeeds when seen as embedded in a composite ground of discrimination. In *Corbiere*, Indian band members challenged a legislative provision which required that band members be 'ordinarily resident' on the reserve in order to vote in band elections as violative of Section 15(1) of the Canadian Charter when less than one third of the registered members of the band lived on the reserve. The Supreme Court found that the legislation was discriminatory based on the analogous ground of 'aboriginality residence', defined both by race and residence as it disadvantaged and stereotyped the non-resident band members. The Court found that residence was a relevant contextual factor as noted in previous cases,[255] but the case of aboriginality-residence was unique and complex to form a separate ground in itself. This was because in this context, aboriginality-residence was transformed into a ground when the two combined to reflect something that fundamentally affected the experience of disadvantage. The two statuses – aboriginality and residence – thus combined to form a ground to be protected from discrimination. The Supreme Court of Canada thus does not seem to have been bothered by the refrain of US courts of not creating 'super categories' or 'new classifications' for the purposes of antidiscrimination law.

Even though a true intersectional claim does not seem to have been either argued explicitly or decided as such by the Supreme Court of Canada, intersectionality seems to have made an inroad in the equality decisions nonetheless. The impact of this is most clear in the decisions handed down by the tribunals that not only follow but develop this line of jurisprudence further. Thus, both the Ontario and the British Columbia Human Rights Tribunals have adjudicated intersectional claims involving a combination of grounds, without falling back on single-axis discrimination in their determination at any point.[256] One

255 *R v Turpin* [1989] 1 SCR 1296.

256 *Morrison v Motsewetsho* (2003) HRTO 21; *Baylis-Flannery v DeWilde* 2003 HRTO 28; *Flamand v DGN Investments* 2005 HRTO 10; *Arias v Desai* 2003 HRTO 1; *Comeau v Cote* (2003) BCHRT 32. See also *Dartmouth Halifax (County) Regional Housing Authority v Sparks* (1993) 119 NSR (2d) 91. Cf *Falkiner v Ontario* (2002) 59 OR (3d) 481 (Ontario Court of Appeal).

example may have to suffice: *Radek v Henderson Development (Canada) Ltd.*[257] The case before the British Columbia Human Rights Tribunal involved a claimant, Gladys Radek, who complained of having been discriminated against on the basis of her race, colour, ancestry and disability. She claimed that the alleged discrimination formed part of a larger pattern of systemic discrimination practised against Aboriginal and disabled people in Canada. The exact facts involved being denied entry and being mistreated by security guards deployed at a mall. The claimant was regularly intercepted by security guards, questioned, and followed around in the mall. She became the target of their attention not only because she was Aboriginal, but also because she walked with a prosthetic leg. In noting the nature of discrimination suffered, the Tribunal explained:

> Ms. Radek has alleged discrimination on the basis of a number of intersecting grounds: race, colour, ancestry and disability. She is a middle-aged Aboriginal woman with a disability. She is multiply disadvantaged on a number of grounds protected by the Code. These grounds cannot be separated out and parsed on an individual basis. Ms. Radek is an integrated person, with a number of characteristics, some of them protected under the Code, all of which are alleged to have been factors in how she was treated on May 10. It is Ms. Radek who went through the events of that day, not a number of disembodied and distinct grounds. Ms. Radek's particulars of allegation reflect this reality in her allegation that she was discriminated against "because of the way I look". The way a person looks is the result of a complex combination of many factors.[258]

The Tribunal's characterisation of the claim is peculiar not only because it breaks away from much of the Supreme Court commentary but also because it maps onto intersectionality scholarship closely. It lists the relevant grounds or identities relevant to the claimant but then asserts their indivisibility in yielding the discrimination experienced. It is firm in its insistence on treating the claimant as 'an integrated person' and not a disembodied version of distinct grounds. It thus appreciated discrimination as experienced by her as a whole and because of 'result of a complex combination of many factors'. But the Tribunal went a step further and recognised that it was not just about the 'grounds' that the claimant alleged as the basis of discrimination but the whole

257 (2005) BCHRT 302 (British Columbia Human Rights Tribunal).
258 Ibid. [463].

context of her personal and socio-economic circumstances that mattered. It thus noted:

> Ms. Radek is also economically disadvantaged. She has a limited income. She lives "on disability" and required subsidized housing. She lives in the Downtown Eastside. Poverty and economic circumstances are not prohibited grounds of discrimination under the Code. Nonetheless, Ms. Radek's economic circumstances were part of who she was and how she presented on May 10. They are integrally interrelated with Ms. Radek's identity as an Aboriginal, disabled woman.[259]

The Tribunal shows extraordinary awareness of the composition of discrimination, which was not confined to a single ground but extended to multiple grounds, as well as, the context in which they operated. Poverty thus becomes a factor that played a role in how discrimination was produced and experienced. In the final analysis, the Tribunal issued an important dicta in examining discrimination claims: '[t]he prohibited ground or grounds of discrimination need not be the *sole or the major factor* leading to the discriminatory conduct; it is sufficient if they are a factor; … The prohibited ground or grounds need not be *the cause* of the respondent's discriminatory conduct; it is sufficient if they are a factor or operative element.'[260] The wording of the dicta, although distinct from the sociological narrative in which intersectionality literature has developed, is distinctively legal and intersectional in fact. It translates intersectionality's main premises into the vernacular of discrimination law ably and issues a clear guiding principle for discrimination lawyers, judges and scholars to work with.

#### 3.1.4 South Africa

South Africa is one the most progressive jurisdictions (even if not the first) in acknowledging that discrimination need not always be based on a single ground. This possibility is alluded to in Section 9 of the South African Constitution. Clause (3) enumerates the constitutional guarantee against discrimination and provides a non-exhaustive list of grounds recognising that discrimination can take place on 'one or more' of these. Such discrimination can be either direct or indirect under clause (4) and is presumed to be unfair when based on enumerated grounds under clause (5). There are several possible ways of classifying the South African jurisprudence under section 9. No

259 Ibid. [467].
260 Ibid. [482].

matter how one approaches the jurisprudence, what is clear is that intersectionality is often easily and readily spotted by the South African courts. This is in contrast with almost every other jurisdiction. But, first, even where the South African Constitutional Court explicitly acknowledges intersectionality, it may not choose to address it as such, but in other ways, i.e. as in Canada using multiple identities as 'context'; or as a matter 'substantially' covered by a single ground; or sometimes even multiple or additive discrimination. And yet, secondly, the Constitutional Court has also recognised and actually addressed intersectionality as is. Both themes deserve unravelling.

The first prominent theme in South African case law relates to the trend of finding discrimination to be 'substantially' based on one enumerated ground. This trend can be attributed to *Brink v Kitshoff*,[261] which was the first case brought under the non-discrimination guarantee of the interim constitution in 1996. The constitutional question involved the validity of the Insurance Act 1943. It was argued that the impugned Act discriminated against married women by depriving them, in certain circumstances, of all or some of the benefits of life insurance policies made in their favour by their husbands. O'Regan J explained the claim as:

> Sections 44(1) and (2) of the Act treat married women and married men differently. This difference in treatment disadvantages married women and not married men. The discrimination in sections 44(1) and (2) is therefore based on two grounds: sex and marital status. Section 8(2) does not require that the discrimination be based on one ground only; it specifically states that it may be based on 'one or more' grounds. Nor is it a difficulty for the applicant that section 8(2) mentions only one of the grounds, sex. The list provided in section 8(2) is not exhaustive. The subsection states expressly that the list provided should not be used to derogate from the *generality of the prohibition on discrimination*.[262]

This acknowledgement is a leap forward from the US and UK jurisprudence that limits the general guarantees of non-discrimination to either a single ground or two grounds at most. The presence of a non-exhaustive list of grounds and a non-discrimination guarantee which explicitly provides for discrimination to be based on 'one or more' of them, enables this reasoning plainly. However, in finding that the impugned provision was discriminatory, O'Regan J was quick to indicate that:

261 *Brink v Kitshoff NO* 1996 (4) SA 197 (CC).
262 Ibid. [43] (emphasis supplied).

> It is not necessary to consider whether the other ground of discrimination, marital status, would be a ground which would constitute unfair discrimination for the purposes of section 8. It is sufficient that the disadvantageous treatment is *substantially based on one of the listed prohibited grounds*, namely, sex.[263]

Thus, despite acknowledging the possibility of using multiple grounds in a discrimination claim, the approach was ultimately one basing the claim on substantially one of the listed grounds. Subsequent cases show considerable allegiance to this approach. The approach is not detrimental for cases that succeed anyway (viz. *Brink*). However, it is certainly not an intersectional approach since it reduces multiple grounds to a single ground in fact. It is as if Black women's claims are admitted no doubt, but as a species of either race *or* sex discrimination but not *both*. The approach is particularly unhelpful when at least one of those characteristics may be considered 'privileged' but actually plays a part in how disadvantage comes about based on its interaction with another. The case of *Hugo* is a good example of this.[264] It involved a discrimination challenge to the Presidential decision granting clemency to all women prisoners with minor children below twelve years of age. The claimant was a single father with a minor child below twelve years of age and his own position demonstrated that it was not just his sex/gender as a male which was formative but also the fact that he was a single father that dictated his experience of discrimination. However, the Constitutional Court classified the issue as substantially a matter of sex discrimination in these terms:

> The Presidential Act, in fact, discriminates on a combined basis, sex coupled with parenthood of children below the age of twelve. Only women who are parents of such children were released: women without children were not. In [*Brink*] this Court held that it is sufficient if the discrimination is substantially based on one of the listed grounds in section 8(2). Accordingly, it is clear that the Presidential Act prima facie discriminates on one of the grounds listed in section 8(2).[265]

The majority upheld the Presidential decision on the basis that 'mothers, as a matter of fact, bear more responsibilities for child-rearing in our society than

---

263 Ibid. (emphasis supplied).

264 *President of the Republic of South Africa and another v Hugo* 1997 (4) SA 1.

265 Ibid. [33].

do fathers'.[266] The reasoning validated the very stereotypes which disadvantage women; but it also validated stereotypes against men, especially those which were just as disadvantaging. It essentialised the notion that men do not provide childcare, unhelpful to those men who were *in fact* primary caregivers, and also those who *could be*, thus upturning the stereotype that only women had to provide childcare. Whilst the Court's observation that women 'as a matter of fact' bore more childcare responsibilities may be true, it is also true that single fathers would bear as much responsibility as women, in addition to emasculating stereotypes attached to caregiving. The absence of a holistic analysis of gender and childcare status frustrated the possibility of identifying patterns of disadvantage that cannot ordinarily be captured by a single ground, in this case, a matter of sex or gender alone. The traditional single ground approach to sex or gender benefits only those for whom disadvantage accrues *solely* on this basis (viz. white middle class non-disabled heterosexual Christian women [not men]) and exclude others for whom sex or gender interacts with other identities of disadvantage like race, colour, religion, marital or parental status in reproducing equally adverse patterns of disadvantage. A 'substantial' focus on one ground like in *Hugo*, blinkers us to other dimensions of people's identities that interact with these grounds in generating patterns of disadvantage, leading to unfair discrimination.[267] *Hugo* is a complex example of how substantial focus on a single ground not just ousts complex forms of discrimination (against single fathers) but also reinforces the stereotypes associated with a ground (sex or gender) and hence fails to remedy such discrimination (against single mothers).

Thus, a substantial focus on one ground has been damaging in cases that could only have succeeded through an appreciation of intersectionality. *Volks v Robinson*[268] is a clear example in this regard. *Volks* involved a provision conferring on surviving spouses the right to claim maintenance from the estates of their deceased spouses if they are not able to support themselves. It was challenged as discriminatory for excluding survivors of stable permanent cohabitation relationships. Mrs Robinson was destitute and wanted to claim from the estate of her deceased partner with whom she had shared a relationship very similar to marriage. Since the claim was pursued as against the constitutionality of a provision which did not afford maintenance to the surviving partner of a permanent life partnership, the Court characterised

266 Ibid. [37].

267 Cathi Albertyn, "Equality" in Cathi Albertyn and Elsje Bonthuys (eds), *Gender, Law and Justice*, Johannesburg, JUTA, 2007, [4-45-4-46].

268 2005 (5) BCLR 446.

the basis of discrimination as one based substantially on 'marital status'. The provision was defended on the basis that: 'the deceased's freedom and dignity would be violated if his fundamental life choices, not to marry and to dispose of his property as he wanted, were to be overridden by a court permitting a maintenance claim against his estate.'[269] However, the evidence in this case was that women in the position of Mrs Robinson, who were economically dependent upon their male partners, had been 'at all times prepared to marry',[270] and in fact did not have this fundamental choice accorded equal dignity during the lifetime of their male partners.[271] The Court wilfully ignored this evidence and chose to focus on the choice of the male partners, a choice which was hugely determined by their gender and socio-economic status. In fact, the Court proceeded with an unreal and overly simplistic explanation of power relations by concluding that Mrs Robinson's 'relationship with Mr Shandling is one in which each was free to continue or not, and from which each was free to withdraw at will, without obligation and without legal or other formalities.'[272] The reality for women like Mrs Robinson was that they are often not the ones who are *free* to choose the form of their relationships due to economic dependence and structural subordination of women in cohabitation relationships. Although, the Court expressed 'genuine concern for vulnerable women who cannot marry despite the fact that they wish to and who become the victims of cohabitation relationships',[273] it disagreed that their situation could be addressed constitutionally.[274]

On the other hand, gender was central to the discrimination inquiry in Sachs J's dissent. According to him:

> The constitutional quest for the achievement of substantive equality therefore requires that patterns of gender inequality reinforced by the law be not viewed simply as part of an unfortunate yet legally neutral background. They are intrinsic, not extraneous, to the interpretive enquiry.[275]

---

269 Ibid. [17].
270 Ibid. [18].
271 Cathi Albertyn, 'Defending and Securing Rights Through Law: Feminism, Law and the Courts in South Africa' (2005) 32 Politikon 217, 229–30; Craig Lind, 'Domestic Partnerships and Marital Status Discrimination' (2005) Acta Juridica 108.
272 Volks (n 268) [55]. Ibid. [55].
273 Ibid. [68].
274 The Court found that the 'answer lies in legal provisions that will make a real difference to vulnerable women at a time when both partners to the relationship are still alive.' Ibid. [68].
275 Ibid. [163].

> … it is women rather than men who in general suffered disadvantage because of their status of being married or not married. Any investigation of unfairness resulting from marital status would accordingly have to take account of the manner in which patriarchy resulted in elements of structured advantage and disadvantage being associated with the status of being and not being married.[276]

However, despite these observations, even Sachs J did not classify the issue as one of discrimination based on more than *one* ground and proceeded with marital status discrimination alone.[277] He did not consider the nature of the claim from the distinct position of female cohabitating partners like Mrs Robinson. He was simply reminding that gender inequality *mattered*. The approach does nothing to understand or address how exactly gender mattered to Mrs Robinson's claim based on marital status in fact.

Another implication of finding discrimination to be based substantially on one ground has been the treatment of claims involving more than one ground as simply multiple or additive discrimination. In fact, the South African Constitutional Court 'has not always been clear of the difference between multiple and intersectional discrimination'[278] and it is useful to see exactly how the two have come muddled. Take for example the case of *Bhe* which involved a constitutional challenge to the rule of male primogeniture in the context of the customary law of succession. The rule was found to be discriminatory because only a male (related to the deceased) qualified as an intestate heir, thus excluding women from intestate succession. The Constitutional Court reached this decision by analysing the effect of the rule based on gender and race separately such that each ground was examined individually to prove discrimination. The Court's analysis moves first to discuss the racist features of the law, then the patriarchal ones. It assumes separate spheres of gender and race discrimination and does not appreciate that discrimination operated quite indistinguishably when the two grounds were fused together in the case of Black women. The approach symbolises multiple discrimination yet again. There are though glimmers of the Court indicating that the discrimination, even if examined separately, seemed to be experienced as one and as embodied in the lives of the claimants, who were economically disadvantaged

276 Ibid. [199].

277 Ibid. [189] ('the legal issue before us is whether the non-inclusion of unmarried cohabitants under the Act violates their constitutional right not to be discriminated against on the ground of marital status.').

278 Albertyn (n 267) [35–53].

women of colour, governed by customary law. Yet, it seems that that assertion is more of an afterthought; giving the impression that discrimination could be *established* individually based on grounds and then *declared* to be adding up to something distinct from individual forms of discrimination experienced on individual grounds. Adding multiple grounds to yield additive discrimination seems to contribute little to recognising intersectionality or to redressing intersectional discrimination in law.

But besides the traditional approaches to complex forms of discrimination highlighted above, the Constitutional Court has been open to developing original ways of approaching discrimination analysis in such cases. The discrimination jurisprudence has repeatedly affirmed its orientation towards understanding the unfavourable *impact* of the discriminatory provision or conduct rather than the purported *aims*. The difficulty in capturing every aspect of the discriminatory experience within the construct of grounds, has led to a focus on claimants' *context*. Context is taken to reflect those identities, statuses and situations which are not captured within the construction of grounds of discrimination. The Constitutional Court has outlined its approach as:

> Discrimination does not take place in discrete areas of the law, hermetically sealed from one another, where each aspect of discrimination is to be examined and its impact evaluated in isolation. *Discrimination must be understood in the context of the experience of those on whom it impacts.*[279]
>
> *One consequence of an approach based on context and impact would be the acknowledgement that grounds of unfair discrimination can intersect,* so that the evaluation of discriminatory impact is done not according to one ground of discrimination or another, but on a combination of both, that is, globally and contextually, not separately and abstractly. The objective is to determine in a qualitative rather than a quantitative way if the group concerned is subjected to scarring of a sufficiently serious nature as to merit constitutional intervention.[280]

The Constitutional Court thus appears to have adopted an approach similar to Canada for going beyond the categorical approach to grounds and the single-axis framework of discrimination. Within the South African contextual approach, even though the basis of discrimination remains a single ground,

---

279 *National Coalition for Gay and Lesbian Equality v Minister of Home Affairs* 2000 (2) SA 1 [35].

280 *National Coalition for Gay and Lesbian Equality and another v Minister of Justice* 1999 (1) SA 6 [113].

every other identity which contributes to the discriminatory impact can be accounted for as context. The approach may be particularly useful in cases with unenumerated grounds or identities which do not instantly qualify as grounds under section 9(3) and thus cannot avail of the presumption of unfair discrimination under section 9(5) which applies to enumerated grounds alone.[281] But the Constitutional Court has even addressed intersectionality as is in the case of *Hassam v Jacobs*,[282] without trying to address it via context, substantially, multiple or additively. It is the approach in *Hassam* that is telling of the possibilities of realising intersectionality in antidiscrimination law and serves as a model in comparative law.

*Hassam* involved a challenge to legislative provisions which excluded widows of Muslim polygynous marriages from intestate succession. The claimant compared her situation to three sets of people whose proprietary interests were protected under the legislative provisions: widows married in terms of the Marriage Act; widows in monogamous Muslim marriages; widows in polygynous customary marriages. By drawing these comparisons, the claimant argued that her exclusion from intestate succession constituted unfair discrimination on the listed grounds of gender, marital status and religion.[283] The claimant pressed for a recognition of intersectional patterns of disadvantage based on grounds of gender, marital status and religion as:

> the failure to include spouses of polygynous Muslim marriages within the ambit of the Act indirectly discriminates against women in those marriages on the ground of gender. This discrimination stems from the reality that women constitute a particularly vulnerable segment of the population and that, in practice, the Act benefits mainly widows rather than widowers. They submitted further that the Act operates to the detriment of Muslim women but not Muslim men because only Muslim men may have multiple spouses under Islamic Law.[284]
>
> discrimination occurs on the ground of marital status in instances where legislative protection is withheld from certain relationships. In withholding certain protections provided for in the Act from persons in

281 *Khosa v Minister of Social Development* 2004 (6) SA 505 and *Hoffmann v South African Airways* 2001 (1) SA 1, are successful examples where the claim was based on unlisted grounds of citizenship and HIV-status and thus did not avail of section 9(5).

282 *Hassam v Jacobs* 2009 (5) SA 572.

283 Ibid. [9].

284 Ibid. [10].

> polygynous Muslim marriages, the applicant submitted that she is being discriminated against on the ground of marital status.[285]
>
> The conclusion of a polygynous Muslim marriage is an element of the right and freedom associated with religious and cultural choices. The failure of the Act to recognise such marriages thus also constitutes discrimination on the ground of religion.[286]

Accepting this analysis, Nkabinde J affirmed that:

> The grounds of discrimination can thus be understood to be overlapping on the grounds of, religion, in the sense that the particular religion concerned was in the past not one deemed to be worthy of respect; marital status, because polygynous Muslim marriages are not afforded the protection other marriages receive; and gender, in the sense that it is only the wives in polygynous Muslim marriage that are affect by the Act's exclusion.[287]

Having identified the 'overlapping' grounds of religion, marital status and gender as the basis of the claim, Nkabinde J found that the grounds lead to unfair discrimination in these terms:

> women in polygynous Muslim marriages still suffer serious effects of non-recognition. The distinction between spouses in polygynous Muslim marriages and those in monogamous Muslim marriages unfairly discriminates between the two groups.[288]
>
> By discriminating against women in polygynous Muslim marriages on the grounds of religion, gender and marital status, the Act clearly reinforces a pattern of stereotyping and patriarchal practices that relegates women in these marriages to being unworthy of protection. Needless to say, by so discriminating against those women, the provisions in the Act conflict with the principle of gender equality which the Constitution strives to achieve.[289]
>
> The purpose of the Act would clearly be frustrated rather than furthered if widows to polygynous Muslim marriages were excluded from

285 Ibid. [11].
286 Ibid. [12].
287 Ibid. [34].
288 Ibid. [36].
289 Ibid. [37].

> the benefits of the Act simply because their marriages were contracted by virtue of Muslim rites. The constitutional goal of achieving substantive equality will not be fulfilled by that exclusion.[290]

Two things make this analysis distinctly intersectional. First, even though three grounds of discrimination were chosen, they were neither considered independently nor were they amalgamated into one. In fact, the purpose of choosing them was to study their intersectional impact or see how patterns of discrimination collide. They were thus considered *as a whole* in respect of the whole of the claimant. Second, the patterns of disadvantage which emerged were considered in their structural sense in terms of how each of them – sexism, marital status discrimination and religious discrimination were co-constituted. The Court showed acute awareness of history and context in examining the particular effects of exclusion for Muslim women in polygynous marriages. They took note of the long history of discrimination against Muslims, especially with respect to marriage; they also noted the particular vulnerable position of women, especially women in polygynous marriages and Muslim women generally, who were socio-economically more vulnerable than women in traditional marriages. The various comparisons within and outside of the groups of Muslims, people in traditional marriages and men, revealed the disadvantage the claimants shared between these groups but also the disadvantage which was peculiar to them. This dynamic of sameness and difference in patterns of group disadvantage – central to intersectionality – was thus appreciated quite comprehensively in *Hassam*. While it may stand alone amongst the antidiscrimination law jurisprudence of apex courts, it certainly shows that intersectional logic is not all that difficult to be absorbed *and* acted upon.

### 3.2 *Scholarship*

Comparative antidiscrimination judicial doctrine leaves us with a sense that while there has been movement away from the traditional form of discrimination conceived along a single axis, intersectionality has not yet displaced single-axis discrimination. This is true of most jurisdictions, and certainly the US, UK, Canada and South Africa. The fact that no single one of them has consistently redressed intersectional discrimination may give the impression that whole of antidiscrimination law has been slow with this. Yet, despite the slow pace of the judicial doctrine, the reality is that antidiscrimination law scholarship has been thriving. The trajectory of the latter is comparable to the

290 Ibid. [38].

trajectory of development of intersectionality theory. It is thus useful to pay attention to it if we want to understand antidiscrimination law as a whole and its disposition towards intersectionality.

The previous part noted that antidiscrimination law scholars had engaged with intersectionality at its peak in the 1970s and 1980s. Importantly, these contributions had preceded Crenshaw's. Shoben's 1981 piece 'Compound Discrimination: The Interaction of Race and Sex in Employment Discrimination' was trendsetting in this regard. The piece was situated well within the Black feminist and critical race discourses, while working with employment decisions of the US courts. Shoben's piece is characteristic of the later scholarship that were to follow, in that it was not a case of intersectionality being originated in or applied to antidiscrimination law only. Intersectionality was being developed in antidiscrimination law while simultaneously being developed in other disciplines across the US. Antidiscrimination law as a site was thus neither the incubator nor the outpost for intersectionality. While its judicial doctrine served as the fulcrum of intersectionality critique, its scholarship served as a key player in how intersectionality came to evolve, and of course, to be eventually christened as such by Crenshaw.

Much the same can be said about antidiscrimination law scholarship elsewhere, which has developed taking cue from the scholarship in the US. Intersectionality has thus developed not only *in* but *through* antidiscrimination law scholarship, despite the record of courts and legislatures on the subject. So important is this contribution in terms of developing intersectionality theory itself that it is vital to examine it on its own.

For example, Crenshaw's initial critique was promptly picked up by her neighbours. So, a familiar critique started to develop in Canada in the early 1990s. Inspired by Crenshaw, Nitya Iyer (earlier Duclos), was one of the first to study the invisibility of racial minority women in Canadian human rights cases.[291] She showed how gender and race of racial minority women went missing in claims of race and sex discrimination respectively, because of the tendency to treat both as separate, mutually exclusive categories, with 'virtually no consideration of the complex interactions of race, sex, and the various other grounds of discrimination that are so much a part of the lived experience (as opposed to the legal analysis) of discrimination.'[292] This kind of analysis, though particularised for racial minority women in Canada, appears characteristic of intersectionality. But Iyer did not just stop at exposing the imposed

291 Nitya Duclos, 'Disappearing Women: Racial Minority Women in Human Rights Cases' (1993) 6 Canadian Journal of Women and the Law 25.

292 Ibid. 40.

invisibility on racial minority women and the complexity of their discrimination. She went on to mount a critique of antidiscrimination law in general by, first, revealing its individualistic nature, and second, arguing against the categorical use of grounds, in these terms:

> The most fundamental error in current antidiscrimination doctrine lies in its location of difference in the individual complainant rather than in his or her *relationship* with others. It treats difference as an intrinsic characteristic of the individual – the discrimination is due to his or her race or sex – rather than as arising out of the relationship between that individual and others. Pinpointing the victim of discrimination as the source of the problem (if it were not for his or her difference, there would be no discrimination) conveniently allows human rights law to maintain an excessively individualistic approach to remedying discrimination, neglecting the systemic and structural causes of discriminatory relationships.[293]
>
> The error in the current approach lies not so much in the use of categories, which may well be intrinsic to the way we think, but in the assumption that the particular categories we are using now are natural, objective, and permanent. We can continue to use the categories we have, in this case the grounds of discrimination, but we should strive to make them flexible, dynamic, and relational.[294]

Iyer's critique of antidiscrimination law thus went broader than Crenshaw's more fundamental critique of the *ways of thinking about discrimination.* Iyer repeated the conceptual critique but then developed it more minutely, exposing how antidiscrimination law's central precepts like grounds were also averse to thinking in intersectional terms. She thus proposed a non-categorical approach to complex claims of discrimination where the claimant 'would merely be required to "assert a particular social identity and show that his or her oppression arises from the hierarchical relationship between the dominant social identity and this identity."'[295] The claimant would thus no longer have to fit prefabricated categories of discrimination but rather assert their own position as one, by showing some kind of a hierarchical relationship between them and others in evidence. The suggestion treads the line of dissent adopted by L'Heureux-Dubé J in cases like *Mossop* and *Egan* and although it has never

293 Ibid. 47 (references omitted).
294 Ibid. 50 (references omitted).
295 Nitya Iyer, 'Categorical Denials: Equality Rights and the Shaping of Social Identity' (1993) 19 Queen's Law Journal 179.

become mainstream, it remains an oft-repeated suggestion from those seeking to make antidiscrimination law respond to intersectional claims specifically. In 1997, Douglos Kropp argued along very similar lines, seeing the potential in L'Heureux-Dubé J's 'put discrimination first' approach which opened the possibilities of adopting a more fluid and complex understanding of identities in antidiscrimination law.[296]

Though not everyone who advocated for intersectionality in antidiscrimination law chose to tread this line. Writing the same year as Iyer, Mary Eaton, criticised L'Heureux-Dubé J's practical approach from *Mossop*, especially the suggestion that discrimination could 'practically' be addressed under a single ground if one or more of the identities involved were not recognised as grounds. L'Heureux-Dubé J was coming from the side that grounds ultimately were not the point of discrimination and her later jurisprudence clearly shows that her focus was more on the context and the reality of discrimination and its impact rather than the technical construct of grounds in antidiscrimination law. Yet, for Eaton, reducing discrimination to a single ground for practical purposes did injustice to intersectionality even if it allowed the claimant to succeed. She explained thus:

> [That] discrimination may be adequately remedied under one head misapprehends the form and shape of complex discrimination. For all three types of oppression, more than symbolic damage is done by reducing an account of "what happened" to unidimensional terms. Law is spared having to engage with the very real injuries of interactive inequalities as they are experienced by multiply oppressed people. Concomitantly, law also reasserts itself as the authoritative interpreter of the social world, and the experience of disempowered groups within it. Thus, the idea that courts can simply deem one or other head as the operative brand of discrimination at issue in any given case is, in other words, a subordinating practice in and of itself.[297]

Eaton's explanation is persuasive in that practicality should not trump other kinds of injustices entailed in reducing a claim based on multiple identities or grounds to one, in order to succeed in courts. Other have adopted this line more firmly, arguing for intersectionality to be recognised as is and not as

296 Douglas Kropp, "Categorical' Failure: Canada's Equality Jurisprudence – Changing Notions of Identity and the Legal Subject' (1997) 23 Queen's Law Journal 201.

297 Mary Eaton, 'At the Intersection of Gender and Sexual Orientation: Towards a Lesbian Jurisprudence' (1994) 3 Southern California Review of Law and Women's Studies 183.

another form of single-ground discrimination. Writing in 2001, with the hindsight of a greater wealth of Canadian equality rights decisions, Dianne Pothier too rejected the formalistic and categorical approaches to grounds, but hesitated to abandon the use of grounds per se.[298] She thus proposed a more 'complicated' approach to grounds wherein the reference to or the use of grounds served as 'a constant reminder' of why discrimination was wrongful. Grounds thus served as the link to understanding discrimination and without a firm understanding of this link, Pothier showed that the discrimination inquiry often ended up being acontextual and fuzzy. According to her, grounds were necessary in appreciating the relational aspect of discrimination and thus making it less abstract. Similar claims were made about the usefulness of the contextual approach to intersectionality: enabling a fuller and more fluid discrimination inquiry that was embedded in grounds but ultimately was not confined to them.[299] This is not to say that the contextual approach was actually able to achieve this. The application of the contextual approach to equality cases not only in Canada but also South Africa, had made it apparent that the existing discourse on contextual approach to discrimination was anything but liberated. But the scholarship was intended to change this discourse pushing towards a truly reformed contextual approach that did what it promised to. This was possible only when context neither replaced nor was limited to grounds. In the words of Small and Grant:

> While different forms of discrimination can and do exacerbate each other and intensify the experience, deriving context merely on the basis of the grounds relied on in any particular case, results in a view of the impact of discrimination in fixed categories, a view which misses the whole picture. Human identities are not fixed, based on imputed group characteristics, but are forged in communities, in complex social interactions. A fully developed contextual approach needs to be able to engage – so far as the litigation process permits – with this complexity.[300]

298 Dianne Pothier, 'Connecting Grounds of Discrimination to Real People's Real Experiences' (2001) 13 Canadian Journal of Women and the Law 37.

299 Carol A Aylward, 'Intersectionality: Crossing the Theoretical and Praxis Divide' (2010) 1 Journal of Critical Race Inquiry 1.

300 Joan Small and Evadné Grant, 'Dignity, Discrimination, and Context: New Directions in South African and Canadian Human Rights Law' (2005) 6 Human Rights Review 25, 48 (references omitted).

Many more concerted efforts for realising intersectionality emerged in the noughties when both intersectionality and antidiscrimination law were under siege, albeit for different reasons. One of the intersectional critiques, as we saw in the last part, was that it was not inclusive enough and perhaps was too focussed on the case of Black women, thus ignoring others who were more privileged in some ways but also disadvantaged in others, viz. gay men. Antidiscrimination law was under siege because it had failed intersectional claimants per se, and not because it had recognised some intersectionality and dismissed others. All intersectional claimants, including minority women, had had it hard as claimants. It was becoming increasingly clear that it was not so much the conceptual resistance to intersectionality but the operation of antidiscrimination law, which was proving to be unwieldy. Judges seemed to *get* intersectionality and their rhetoric reflected as much, but they did not quite know what to *do* with it. As the early critiques of grounds and context had exposed, there were also intractable problems with other aspects like the disregard of indirect discrimination, the requirement of comparison, the use of 'human dignity' as a test of discrimination, the low standard of review, etc. Each of these was being picked up and explored by antidiscrimination scholars.[301]

Emily Carcaso, writing around the same time as Iyer and Eaton in 1993, pressed on the indistinguishability of different axes of discrimination through her own case as a woman of colour academic at a Canadian university.[302] She explored her vulnerability in the context of her employment situation and asserted the impossibility of determining 'whether I believed that I had been discriminated against because of my race or my gender'.[303] This exercise maps onto much of the US scholarship that developed a distinctly ontological understanding of intersectionality by speaking as intersectional subjects, as Black woman, rather than speaking for or about them. But the point of it all was to extend analyses which were personal and affective, to others similarly situated, and to create solidarities for strategic thought and action in antidiscrimination law. Thus, Carcaso explained:

301 Daphne Gilbert and Diana Majury, 'Critical Comparisons: The Supreme Court of Canada Dooms Section 15' (2006) 24 Windsor Year Book of Access to Justice 111; Denise G Réaume, 'The Relevance of Relevance to Equality Rights' (2006) 31 Queen's Law Journal 696; Daphne Gilbert, 'Time to Regroup: Rethinking Section 15 of the Charter' (2003) 48 McGill Law Journal 627.

302 Emily Carasco, 'A Case of Double Jeopardy: Race and Gender' (1993) 6 Canadian Journal Women and Law 142, 152.

303 Ibid. 143.

> Proving systemic discrimination based on gender in my case was made possible by the availability of research and statistics relating to women in Canadian universities. Proving systemic discrimination based on the combination of race and gender would have been a lot more difficult simply because of the paucity of women of colour in Canadian universities and the corresponding lack of salary data. The issue of why there are so few women of colour in law faculties is a whole other story. As a woman of colour, I could not help wondering if it was indeed necessary to prove that other women of colour had been treated in a similar fashion before my own treatment, as a woman of colour, could be acknowledged.[304]

Much along the same lines, Carl F Stychin made the explicit claim of postmodern identity politics being central to the development of antidiscrimination law in Canada.[305] The intervention was helpful not only in extending intersectional readings of identity and antidiscrimination law to Canada, but also to understanding the Canadian context itself more fundamentally. Stychin's claim was particularly with respect to identity politics around nationalism and sexual orientation, themes not dissimilar to those explored in the US but certainly distinct from the central case of Black women in the US. The acceptance of emergent identities, especially those previously ousted like the 'homosexual', were seen as a testament to the progressive possibilities in Canadian antidiscrimination law. Although Stychin was sceptical of the terms on which these possibilities came live, especially the reliance on concepts like immutability and historicity of disadvantage, which did not square with the postmodern understanding of identity as contingent and changing.[306] His plea was thus to use this postmodern understanding to fine-tune equality rights, a common entreaty in intersectional scholarship: suggesting not simply to transcend but transform powerful tools like law, especially antidiscrimination law. The belief that radical theories like intersectionality *can* do this, without being subsumed by or being transmogrified by the power of law, was apparent in early comparative antidiscrimination scholarship as it is now.

Much of this transpired in reference to the early South African jurisprudence where courts, with some exceptions, had failed intersectionality. Thus, scholars were forging comparative links to have a better grasp of the reasons for which antidiscrimination law proved highly resistant to intersectionality, a

304 Ibid. 152.

305 Carl F Stychin, 'A Postmodern Constitutionalism: Equality Rights, Identity Politics, and the Canadian National Imagination' (1994) 17 Dalhousie Law Journal 61.

306 Ibid. 72–73.

fact that seemed to transcend jurisdictions. For example, Grabham explored the coinciding tendencies in the Canadian and South African equality cases that treated intersectionality as a form of discrimination 'akin to defining it as yet another identity, instead of allowing it to question the constitution of the identity subject positions.'[307] Thus, she showed that where recognised, 'intersectional discrimination has often been expressed as a 'new' ground: yet another form of legally intelligible identity.'[308] From an intersectionalist perspective the problem is obvious: if antidiscrimination law's perception of discrimination based on more than one ground is that it is based on a new self-standing ground, the point about *intersection* is lost. This view of antidiscrimination law would then confirm fears of fragmentation of identities ad infinitum to a point there is no identity politics left and no possibility of collective action or solidarity. The critique of this approach in antidiscrimination law thus maps onto the defence of intersectionality against the inevitability of fragmentation. Antidiscrimination scholars thus seemed to be doing a similar thing as intersectionality scholars. In fact, as Crenshaw's own position illustrates the difference between the two – antidiscrimination scholars and intersectionality scholars – is often illusory.[309]

The post-apartheid scholarship in South Africa shows this clearly. The scholarship after the interim and the permanent Constitution has been distinctly intersectional from incipience. This is true not only of equality rights but rights more generally, with intersectionality being a significant concern for all rights and for transformative justice. For our purposes, the scholarship on section 9(3) – the constitutional right to non-discrimination – is particularly relevant. One of the earliest pieces from Cathi Albertyn and Beth Goldblatt in 1998 set the tone for equality scholarship to be oriented, like the rest of the Constitution, towards transformative aims.[310] In exploring what was very much 'indigenous jurisprudence', Albertyn and Goldblatt were acutely aware of the South African context which was rife with intersectionality such that there were no meaningful categories like 'women' or 'minorities' in South Africa

307 Emily Grabham, 'Intersectionality: Traumatic Impressions' in Grabham et al. (n 126) 193.

308 Ibid.

309 The same holds true for the lawyer/scholar divide, which is illusory in practice, especially of antidiscrimination law. The reference to 'scholars' here is only to indicate that the focus is on the written word of lawyering which is often published as books and journal articles, rather than court briefs or legal opinions, which may be equally scholarly.

310 Cathi Albertyn and Beth Goldblatt, 'Facing the Challenge of Transformation: Difficulties in the Development of an Indigenous Jurisprudence of Equality' (1998) 14 South African Journal on Human Rights 248.

without reference, also to class, region, religion, ethnicity, marital status etc. Relying explicitly on Crenshaw, they opined thus:

> The intersectional nature of disadvantage (based on more than one ground) is therefore complex, creating different and multiple forms of inequality which cannot be explained or understood simply by reference to one of the grounds, such as gender. Sensitivity to context also requires sensitivity to the intricate and compounding nature of disadvantage. These critical insights point to an equality jurisprudence which places difference and disadvantage at the centre of the concept. They point to the importance of the relationship of the individual to the group and the often complicated and intersectional nature of inequalities that are found in reality. They insist on the remedial purpose of the right and the contextual nature of its determination. We believe that such an understanding of equality is most appropriate for South Africa's Constitutional project.[311]

Despite such detailed direction, the South African Constitutional Court's doctrine did not (always) follow either an intersectional or a transformative path. Thus, writing after decisions like *Volks*, Elsje Bonthuys criticised the Court's neglect of intersectionality which had proved to be detrimental to Black and poor women. In her opinion, '[t]he tone for the Constitutional Court's treatment of intersectional grounds of discrimination was, to a certain extent, set by O'Regan J.'s judgment in the *Brink* case ... When faced with intersectional grounds of discrimination, the court tends to focus on one of the grounds or to separate the grounds from one another, rather than examining the disadvantage caused by the interaction between them.'[312] The loss was substantive. Taking the example of *Volks*, Bonthuys showed:

> The failure to argue intersectional discrimination on the bases of marital status, gender, race, and class allowed the majority to base its judgment on the positions of those women who have the choice of whether or not to marry. Although the judgment would not materially affect the position of such privileged women, it would impact on those women cohabitants who do not have similar choices. It also impedes the chances of success

311 Ibid. 253.

312 Elsje Bonthuys 'Institutional Openness and Resistance to Feminist Arguments: The Example of the South African Constitutional Court' (2008) 20 Canadian Journal of Women and Law 1, 26.

> for future maintenance claims by cohabitants or claims to share in assets amassed during the cohabitation relationship.[313]

Her suggestion was thus:

> A proper understanding and theoretical formulation of intersectionality is particularly important in South Africa because our society was, and still remains, so profoundly marked by race, economic class, culture, and religion. In South Africa, there are no "women." There are only black women, Muslim women, white women, women living in poverty, women subject to customary law, and so on. If the courts fail to perceive how these factors interact, there is a serious risk that they will fail to alleviate the oppression of the majority of women.[314]

Marius Pieterse issued a similar call having critiqued the Constitutional Court's approach in cases like *Volks* and *Bhe*.[315] For Pieterse, a less formal approach to grounds, similar to that of Iyer's, was preferable in South Africa too. But that was not enough, Pieterse showed how other aspects of the discrimination inquiry required some work too, including the dignity-based test, which was too oversimplified and often failed to recognise violations that should matter, viz. *Hugo*. The push to reform antidiscrimination law wholesale to accommodate intersectionality seems to have thus gained ground within just a decade of the South African Constitutional Court's output on equality rights. The present decade certainly does not seem to match this output in any measure and perhaps explains why equality jurisprudence too has instead focussed on issues which are moot before the courts, viz. affirmative action etc.[316] Scholarship does map onto judicial doctrine in that sense and it is clear that the push for intersectionality becomes more strategic and ground-level, focussed on policy, social movements etc., when courts' engagement with it wanes. As the remarkable Rhodes Must Fall and Fees Must Fall movements in South Africa show, there is no doubt that intersectionality continued to develop in other spheres; but it is clear that there has been less of an intersectional focus in both antidiscrimination scholarship and judicial doctrine (the former because of the lack of latter perhaps) in the last decade.

313 Ibid. 28.

314 Ibid. 29.

315 Marius Pieterse, 'Finding for the Applicant? Individual Equality Plaintiffs and Group-based Disadvantage' (2008) 24 South African Journal on Human Rights 397.

316 *South African Police Service v Solidarity obo Barnard* [2014] ZACC 23, 2014 (6) SA 123 (CC), 2014 (10) BCLR 1195.

In line with the Canadian and South African scholarship, the UK too began its conversation on intersectionality in antidiscrimination law in the early 1990s. Much of this early exploration was in the context of labour law, from which equality or antidiscrimination as a field developed in the UK. Diamond Ashiagbor presented a carefully studied example of part-time and domestic workers in the UK who were predominantly BAME woman.[317] Their vulnerability could only be understood in reference to class and cultural backgrounds, in addition to their gender, immigration status and race taken as a whole. One of the earliest pieces from Sandra Fredman and Erika Szyszczak in 1992 had also explored the interaction of race and gender.[318] They showed considerable scepticism in reducing claims of intersectionality, which were synergistic in nature, to additive discrimination that they understood to be a discrimination taken as the sum of individual parts (grounds). The latter was, they argued, all too common, and not only in the UK. Using comparative references, especially the example of the South African Constitutional Court's decision in *Bhe*, Fredman and Szyszczak delineated the harm of failing to treat intersectional claimants 'as whole persons' in antidiscrimination law.[319] Thus, not only were intersectional claims failing conceptually and remedially, but there were recognition or expressive harms involved too.[320] Scholars were quick to call out this treatment of intersectional claimants. Emily Grabham found that the antidiscrimination discourse implicated lawyers and their clients 'in essentializing processes that "lose" the complexities of lived experiences.'[321] Similarly, Aileen McColgan, writing after the *Bahl* decision, called out the Court of Appeal's approach which construed Dr Bahl as simply too different from the norm:

> Not only does the decision in Bahl protect intersectional discrimination from challenge under domestic discrimination law, it renders proof of discrimination virtually impossible for someone who differs from the "unstated norm" in more than one respect, unless she avoids drawing attention to more than one of her deviations from this norm.[322]

317 Diamond Ashiagbor, 'The Intersection Between Gender and "Race" in the Labour Market' in S Seldon (ed), *Feminist Perspectives on Employment Law* (Cavendish 1998).

318 Sandra Fredman and Erika Szyszczak, 'The Interaction of Race and Gender' in Bob Hepple and Erika Szyszczak (eds), *Discrimination: The Limits of the Law* (Mansell 1992). See also Nicola Lacey, 'From Individual to Group' in the same volume.

319 Fredman and Szyszczak, ibid. 223.

320 A point later picked up and argued in detail by Gay Moon in 'Multiple Discrimination: Justice for the Whole Person' (2009) 2 Journal of the European Roma Rights Centre 5.

321 Grabham (n 138).

322 McColgan, 'Reconfiguring Discrimination Law' (n 219) 81.

The UK scholarship *truly* caught onto intersectionality in the lead up to the new Equality Act 2010. The scholarship preceding the consolidated equality legislation had started to show the neglect of intersectionality and its consequences. This no doubt played a role in advocating for the provision on 'combination discrimination' in Section 14 but its continued lack of enforcement in the ten years of operation of the Equality Act, is telling of the deep resistance towards intersectional claims.[323] Scholarship has responded to such resistance in very specific terms. Like elsewhere, while the primary resistance has been conceptual in nature: in thinking about discrimination as confined to a single axis alone; the practical hurdles have been equally (or more) bothersome. One of the most significant problems was the existence of separate legislations on each ground individually: Equal Pay Act 1970, Sex Discrimination Act 1975, Race Relations Act 1976, and Disability Discrimination Act 1995. As the experience in *Bahl* had shown, this regime was nearly unworkable for intersectional claimants, who were arguing across legislations and on grounds like age, sexual orientation, religion etc., which were not protected at all. Sarah Hannett, writing for the Oxford Journal of Legal Studies in 2003,[324] argued that this regime was both overly broad and yet under-inclusive at the same time, because:

> Both conceptually and practically, each discrete ground (race, sex and disability) is over-broad, as each is presented as embodying *all* the adverse treatment suffered by a claimant, even where the claimant feels that the discrimination suffered was based on more than one social characteristic ... Second, the grounds of anti-discrimination law are under-inclusive. Where a claimant alleges multiple discrimination, and one ground is unprotected, for example, sexual orientation, this may affect not only the success of the multiple discrimination claim, but also the outcome of the discrimination claim on the protected ground, for example sex.[325]

323 Not everyone agreed though that reform could achieve equality in a greater, intersectional sense, especially via the structure of antidiscrimination law. See Joanne Conaghan, 'Intersectionality and UK Equality Initiatives' (2007) 23 South African Journal on Human Rights 317. Though she qualified her skepticism as: 'This is not to suggest that we should settle for less than the best law has to offer; but it is to acknowledge that the best law has to offer falls far short of solving the problem of inequality on its own.' Ibid. 332.

324 Sarah Hannett, "Equality at the Intersections: The Legislative and Judicial Failure to Tackle Multiple Discrimination" (2003) 23 Oxford Journal of Legal Studies 65.

325 Ibid. 72 (emphasis supplied).

Another frequent hurdle has been that of comparison, which is indispensable in proving discrimination under UK law.[326] Scholars have consistently critiqued the overreliance on comparators, especially in claims based on more than one ground, which seem to fail at this level with astonishing frequency. Hannett critiqued this requirement for being too burdensome for intersectional claimants who find it difficult to either find a comparator or choose between possible comparator groups. But the problem is not just that. Sure enough, the number and choice of comparators do pose a problem worth cracking in intersectional discrimination. But it is rather the sheer necessity and the ultimate usefulness of comparison that is questionable; that discrimination *must* be proven via comparison does not quite ensure that we understand anything about *discrimination* per se, at least in a substantive sense.[327] The push towards loosening the comparator requirement has since been successful, both in Canada and the UK. Yet, it does not always seem to help in the proof of intersectional discrimination, which may (ironically) require greater attention to comparative aspects but not in the rigid form of the comparator test. Scholarship continues to probe this point across jurisdictions since comparators continue to be invoked in cases involving multiple grounds.[328]

Iyiola Solanke's extensive consideration of intersectionality in UK antidiscrimination law has been similarly comprehensive. In her 2009 article, she critiqued UK courts' treatment of intersectionality not only conceptually, or 'qualitatively' as she put it; but also, severally in terms of antidiscrimination law's test for analogous grounds embedded in immutability, and an acontextual approach to discrimination analysis.[329] In her 2017 monograph, she made an even bigger intervention and argued for a theoretical approach to discrimination conceived particularly to address intersectional discrimination.[330] This was based on her anti-stigma principle, proposed as an overarching theory of discrimination capable of accommodating both individual and structural cases of discrimination, especially those of intersectional discrimination and based on more than one ground.

326 This is a legislative requirement in the way direct and indirect discrimination are defined specifically in sections 13 and 19, and also section 14 on combination discrimination in the Equality Act 2000. This is a carryover from previous discrimination legislations (except DDA) which defined discrimination in comparative terms. See SDA, s 5(3); RRA, s 3(4).

327 Aileen McColgan, 'Cracking the Comparator Problem: Discrimination, "Equal" Treatment and The Role of Comparisons' (2006) European Human Rights Law Review 650.

328 Shreya Atrey, 'Comparison in Intersectional Discrimination' [2018] Legal Studies 379.

329 Iyiola Solanke, 'Putting Race and Gender Together: A New Approach to Intersectionality' (2009) 72 Modern Law Review 723.

330 Iyiola Solanke, *Discrimination as Stigma: A Theory of Anti-discrimination Law* (Hart 2016).

My own recent treatment of the subject in *Intersectional Discrimination* taps into these wide-ranging interventions that concern theory and practice of intersectionality in antidiscrimination law together but granularly. The effort therein is not only to show what intersectionality is and what antidiscrimination law has done about it, but also to show how it can be done right in antidiscrimination law. The fact that the latter is still needed shows just how divergent antidiscrimination law has been in comparison to intersectionality; that thirty years after Crenshaw's intervention in the field there still is no roadmap for its success in antidiscrimination law. But at least antidiscrimination scholarship appears to be in sync with intersectionality, and confirms intersectionality's continuing relevance in a field waiting to be transformed.

## Conclusion

The review of the fields of intersectionality theory and antidiscrimination law is an exercise in appreciating the long and resistant relationship between the two. Obviously, the intersection of the two cannot be studied until the trajectory of how the intersection came about is studied. It is only when intersectionality and its rich history of development is appreciated, that one can make sense of its intersection with antidiscrimination law. That is because the reason why intersectionality's relationship with antidiscrimination law matters, coincides with the reason why intersectionality itself matters. All of this very circular logic may seem cumbersome, but it is perhaps the point, that the fields are all too related – their paths crisscross and merge indistinguishably.

But much as the two fields have in fact been interacting this way, the result is not a merging of fields but a somewhat fortification of each. Comparative references from across jurisdictions show that intersectional logic may not have escaped antidiscrimination law, but it has not seeped into it either. Intersectionality on the other hand continues to develop as a field of studies, but not without its own experience of being resisted, and not only from antidiscrimination law. Critiques of intersectionality have mounted a considerable challenge to the field, but it survives, in fact thrives, with ever stronger defences. While intersectionality resists being diluted, appropriated, rejected, obviated, co-opted etc.; antidiscrimination law in turn resists intersectionality and being transformed in turn. The difference between the two is plainly this: that the former is resisting as a critical theory of social change, and latter is resisting the critical theory of change itself. So, while the citadel-like structure makes sense for one (intersectionality), it seems misguided in the case of the other (antidiscrimination law).

This metaphorical ending could appear too cynical, especially of the possibilities of a more merged future of intersectionality and antidiscrimination law, or specifically the realisation of intersectionality in antidiscrimination law. In laying bare the reality of the contemporary discourse, the article in fact hopes to do the opposite. In particular, I hope the reader takes away a sense of what is lost when the sophistication of intersectionality theory is not translated into antidiscrimination law. Thirty years after Crenshaw's seminal piece, we only have a foot in the door in penetrating the antidiscrimination law foothold. All the more reason to continue to break in more closely, as in fact antidiscrimination law scholarship does; and as the scholarship on intersectionality theory shows, these struggles may be protracted, but never in vain.

www.ingramcontent.com/pod-product-compliance
Lightning Source LLC
Chambersburg PA
CBHW031331230926
51848CB00001B/193
* 9 7 8 9 0 0 4 3 8 2 8 4 8 *